The Quality of Our Financial Markets

Zicklin School of Business Financial Markets Series

Robert A. Schwartz, Editor

Zicklin School of Business
Baruch College CUNY
New York, NY, USA

Other Books in the Series:

Schwartz, Robert A., Byrne, John A., Schnee, Gretchen (eds.):
Rethinking Regulatory Structure
Schwartz, Robert A., Byrne, John A., Colaninno, Antoinette (eds.):
Volatility
Schwartz, Robert A., Byrne, John A., Colaninno, Antoinette (eds.):
Technology and Regulation
Schwartz, Robert A., Byrne, John A., Colaninno, Antoinette (eds.):
Competition in a Consolidating Environment
Schwartz, Robert A., Byrne, John A., Colaninno, Antoinette (eds.):
The New NASDAQ Marketplace
Schwartz, Robert A., Byme, John A., Colaninno, Antoinette (eds.):
Electronic vs. Floor Based Trading
Schwartz, Robert A., Byrne, John A., Colaninno, Antoinette (eds.):
Coping with Institutional Order Flow
Schwartz, Robert A., Byrne, John A.. Colaninno, Antoinette (eds.):
A Trading Desk View of Market Quality
Schwartz, Robert A., Byrne, John A., Colaninno, Antoinette (eds.):
Call Auction Trading: New Answers to Old Questions
Schwartz, Robert A. (ed.):
Regulation of Equity Markets

For further volumes:
http://www.springer.com/series/7133

Robert A. Schwartz • John Aidan Byrne
Gretchen Schnee
Editors

The Quality of Our Financial Markets

Taking Stock of Where We Stand

Springer

Editors
Robert A. Schwartz
Speiser Professor of Finance
Zicklin School of Business
Baruch College CUNY
New York, NY, USA

John Aidan Byrne
New York, NY, USA

Gretchen Schnee
Zicklin School of Business
Baruch College, CUNY
New York, NY, USA

ISBN 978-1-4614-5591-2 ISBN 978-1-4614-5592-9 (eBook)
DOI 10.1007/978-1-4614-5592-9
Springer New York Heidelberg Dordrecht London

Library of Congress Control Number: 2012947402

Printed on acid-free paper

Springer is part of Springer Science+Business Media (www.springer.com)

Preface
Quality of Our Financial Markets

Opening Remarks: Robert Schwartz, *Speiser Professor of Finance, Zicklin School of Business, Baruch College, CUNY*

Financial markets on both sides of the Atlantic have changed irrevocably and, in recent years, these markets have entered a brave new world. Here are some extraordinary highlights: The NASDAQ Marketplace and the NYSE have been reengineered. Numerous alternative markets have arrived on the scene. In the USA, for instance, the number of these so-called Alternative Trading Systems, or ATSs, has reached epic proportions, some 41. We have transitioned from a much slower, human-intermediated, relatively consolidated marketplace to a much faster, more dis-intermediated – and considerably more fragmented – marketplace. Not so many years ago, the speed of trading was measured in seconds, a slow trot by today's standards! Today, trading time is measured in milliseconds. Not so many years ago, the NYSE's market share of trading in its own listed stock was over 80 %; today it is about 30 %. At the same time, we have evolved from fairly gray markets at both the NYSE and NASDAQ to a mélange of very lit markets and very dark markets.

What accounts for the changing dynamics of the markets? It is in good part attributable to computer technology. Yet technology is not the only driver. Regulation has also had a profound impact. Here are some highlights in the US markets, starting in 1997: The SEC's Order Handling Rules (1997), Reg ATS (1998), the switch from fractional stock price increments to minimum increments of a penny by 2001, and Regulation NMS (2005).

What is the effect of these changes on market quality? In one sense, it all sounds very good. Commissions have fallen, spreads have tightened and, from the evidence that I have seen, market impact costs have decreased. All this suggests that market quality has improved. But has it really improved? This is the fundamental question and the focus of this book – and the accompanying Baruch College conference, The Quality of Our Financial Markets, hosted on October 19, 2010.

To address the issue of market quality, let's first consider what the term means. Does it refer only to trading costs as conventionally measured? That is, commissions, spreads, and market impact? To answer this, let's agree on what it is that a market actually does, on the economic function that a market performs. I suggest four things:

1. Handle transactions with reasonable speed, at reasonable cost
2. Quantity discovery
3. Price discovery
4. Facilitate capital raising in the primary markets

1. *Handling transactions:* The conventional measures of transaction costs (commissions, spreads, and market impact) pertain to this. They pertain to the liquidity of a market. They of course are important. Enough said for now on this one.
2. *Quantity discovery:* This refers to the process of large buyers and large sellers finding each other. This search is related to what the three Nobel Laureates in economics in 2010 (Peter A. Diamond, Dale T. Mortensen, and Christopher A. Pissarides) have looked at in relation to labor markets and other much slower markets. How readily do unemployed workers and employers with job vacancies find each other? Why does unemployment persist in the face of job vacancies? Equity traders with large orders trade in blocks or slice and dice them. Either way, how effectively do they find each other and trade at reasonable prices? How well is quantity discovery integrated with price discovery? Have these two important processes been decoupled unduly?
3. *Price discovery:* Accurate price discovery is exceedingly important, not just for the participants in a trade. It is also exceedingly important for a far broader array of people to whom market-established prices matter. Prices are used for a variety of legal valuation purposes: for marking-to-market, for converting mutual fund inflows or withdrawals into fund holdings or cash, for performance benchmarks for institutional traders, and for derivative trading and settlements. Also, I add, market-established prices are used for academic research on stock returns.

I wish to expand on price discovery. I have emphasized price discovery at a number of our conferences, and have long focused on it in my research. In neither academic research nor regulatory policy has price discovery, in my opinion, received anywhere near sufficient attention. A major reason is that the values of prices that a market is seeking to discover are not observable.

Think of the unobservable price as a balance price for the market or, in microeconomic parlance, as an equilibrium value. Think of it as a value that the market is continually searching for, groping for, but never really knows where it is. If an equilibrium price is not observable, how can we assess the size of the deviations from this magic number?

Actually, we can do it. Inaccuracies in price discovery that we call noise leave their footprints in the transaction record. They do so because price discovery, as a protracted process, accentuates intra-day price volatility. Recognizing this, let's look at one time during the trading day when price discovery, on a daily basis, is particularly challenging. Consequently, prices are particularly volatile during this period. Let's look at the opening minutes of trading.

I have done this with two colleagues, Jim Ross, a frequent participant in these conferences, and Nazli Sila Alan, one of our stellar Baruch doctoral students, whose Ph.D. dissertation I am sponsoring. We have tracked the evolution of opening volatility on a daily basis, from January 4, 1993 to the current time. Here is the bottom line on this research which is still in process: For the 27 NYSE listed Dow Stocks, we find that volatility in the opening and closing minutes of trading is considerably higher now than it was at the beginning of our sample period. Moreover, opening volatility has itself become considerably more volatile.[1]

4. *Capital raising in the primary markets:* This function is tremendously important. The interaction between the new issues markets and the secondary markets for already issued shares has deteriorated critically in recent years. For an in-depth analysis of this, I call your attention to a June 2010 Grant Thornton publication by David Weild and Edward Kim entitled *Market Structure is Causing the IPO Crisis – and More.*

The number of IPOs overall has declined, led by a plunge in the number of IPOs for small companies. What accounts for this? According to Weild and Kim, the cause is market structure:

> The IPO Crisis is primarily a market-structure-caused crisis, the roots of which date back at least to 1997

They added:

> … the erosion of the U.S. IPO market can be seen as the… unintended consequences… of uncoordinated regulatory changes and inevitable technology advances – all of which stripped away the economic model that once supported investors and small cap companies with capital commitment, sales support and high-quality research.

Steve Wunsch, in the October 11 issue of *Barron's*, tells a similar story:

> One consequence, made rudely visible in the Flash Crash of May 6, is that our markets are now less stable. … NMS appears to have destroyed the human ecosystem that once made capital-raising attractive and profitable.

Wunsch's assertion that our markets are now less stable is clearly supported, I will add, by my empirical volatility analysis with Alan and Ross.

I view the broad marketplace, including the secondary market and the new share issuance market, as an ecology that comprises a rich spectrum of participants. Their motives for trading, investing, and capital raising can vary immensely. But the different parts need each other to function. They need each other to establish quotes, to realize trades, and to raise capital.

New technology and the new regulatory environment have changed the ecology. In so doing, they have profoundly affected market quality. Market quality is multifaceted

[1]Since the conference, the study has been extended to cover the period January 4, 1993 to December 31, 2010, and the sample expanded to include 50 large NYSE stocks and 50 large NASDAQ stocks.

and complex. Could it be that the current ecological structure of the marketplace, with its tighter spreads and lower commissions, is not working so well for the broad market? We must get to the bottom of this as a matter of priority. After all, the consequences for the country's economic growth and employment prospects are far reaching.

List of Participants

Name	Organization	Title
Stuart Adams	FIX Protocol Ltd.	FPL EMEA Regional Director
Paul Britton	Capstone Holdings Group	CEO
Andrew Brooks	T. Rowe Price Associates, Inc.	Vice President and Head of U.S. Equity Trading
Ari Burstein	Investment Company Institute	Senior Counsel – Securities Regulation
Kevin Callahan	X41 Trading, LLC	CEO
Joseph Cangemi	ConvergEx	Managing Director
Alfred Eskandar	Liquidnet	Head of Equities
Reto Francioni	Deutsche Börse AG	CEO
Robert Gasser	ITG	CEO
Jim Gatheral	Weissman School of Arts and Sciences, Baruch College, CUNY	Professor
Susan Greenglass	Ontario Securities Commission	Director Market Regulation
Alan Hill	Jones Trading Institutional Services	CFO
Marcus Hooper	Pipeline Financial Group Ltd.	Head of European Business & Executive Director
Gary Katz	International Securities Exchange	President & CEO
Richard Ketchum	FINRA	Chairman and CEO
Marie Konstance	Nomura Securities International, Inc.	Executive Director Electronic Trading Services
Charles-Albert Lehalle	CA Cheuvreux Credit Agricole Investment Bank	Head of Quantitative Research
Matt Lyons	Capital Research and Management Company	Global Trading Manager
Tim Mahoney	BIDS Trading	CEO

(continued)

(continued)

Name	Organization	Title
Mary McDermott-Holland	NASDAQ OMX*At the time of the conference, Mary McDermott-Holland was with NASDAQ OMX	VP – Transaction Services
Joe Mecane	NYSE Euronext	EVP, Co-Head of US Listing and Cash Execution
Doreen Mogavero	Mogavero, Lee & Company	President & CEO
William O'Brien	Direct Edge	CEO
David Palmer	Hudson Bay Capital Management	Portfolio Manager – Volatility
Jim Ross	Financial Markets Horizons *At the time of the conference, Jim Ross was with Financial Markets Horizons	CEO
Lawrence Ryan	Hewlett-Packard	Chief Technologist
Justin Schack	Rosenblatt Securities, Inc.	Director of Market Structure Analysis
Robert Schwartz	Zicklin School of Business, Baruch College, CUNY	Speiser Professor of Finance
Rob Shapiro	Bloomberg Tradebook LLC	Global Head of Execution Consulting
Cameron Smith	Quantlab Financial, LLC	Executive Vice President, General Counsel
Joseph Wald	Knight Direct LLC	Managing Director

Conference Sponsors

BIDS Trading
Bloomberg Tradebook LLC
Direct Edge
Hewlett-Packard
International Securities Exchange
ITG
Jones Trading Institutional Services
Liquidnet
NASDAQ OMX
NYSE Euronext
Pipeline Trading Systems

Contents

Chapter 1
High-Frequency Trading: Friend or Foe?

Moderator: Jim Gatheral, *Baruch College, CUNY*
Ari Burstein, *Investment Company Institute*
Kevin Callahan, *X41 Trading, LLC*
Charles-Albert Lehalle, *CA Cheuvreux Credit Agricole Investment Bank*
Doreen Mogavero, *Lee & Company*
Lawrence Ryan, *Hewlett-Packard*
Cameron Smith, L, *Quantlab Financial, LLC*

JIM GATHERAL: Let me ask the obvious question: High-frequency trading: friend or foe?

ARI BURSTEIN: Actually, the question should be, "Certain market practices associated with high-frequency: trading: friend or foe?" Let me explain. We at the ICI are not necessarily trying to focus on a particular market participant. We don't really have a problem with high-frequency trading per se. Then again, depending on how you define high-frequency trading, or HFT, everybody does high-frequency or high-speed trading, including mutual funds.

However, we are looking at the practices in the markets lately like canceled orders. Are they good or bad? What about certain HFT strategies such as gaming long-term investors? What about other things that are associated with high-frequency trading – co-location, sponsored access, market data feeds and issues like that? I am hearing from the mutual funds industry that canceled orders are an issue. What is market manipulation? When do you cross the line from a certain strategy into market manipulation? What is liquidity? Is it there for a millisecond and then it disappears? Is that true liquidity? Is that liquidity beneficial to institutional investors? Friend or foe? Is there information out there to really make that decision? Is there enough transparency about high-frequency trading, the practices, about how much of the volume high-frequency traders are, what names they are in? And so on and so forth.[1]

[1] In an interview with *Traders Magazine*, Burstein elaborated at length about the position of the ICI on high-frequency trading. He told the trade publication: "HFTs are not doing anything illegal. They are taking advantage of inefficiencies in the market structure. Institutions, for better or worse, try to hide their orders to prevent leakage of information. Everybody's trying to sniff out everybody's orders. We don't have a problem with that. Our concern is transparency and the needs of regulators. We have issues where there is abuse or manipulative practices. Regulators are having difficulties detecting this because of a lack of transparency. That's where we want to see some changes." Ari Burstein Discusses, *Traders Magazine*, January 21, 2011, http://www.tradersmagazine.com/news/ici-burstein-hft-buyside-106950-1.html

R.A. Schwartz et al. (eds.), *The Quality of Our Financial Markets: Taking Stock of Where We Stand*, Zicklin School of Business Financial Markets Series,
DOI 10.1007/978-1-4614-5592-9_1,

KEVIN CALLAHAN: Whether you are a buy-side or sell side-trader, the high-frequency trader can be both your friend and foe. Let's say you have a smaller order, a small percent of the Average Daily Volume (ADV). If, for example, you only have a total of one hundred shares to execute to complete your order, then the high-frequency trader can be your friend. In this instance, the HFT traders will provide you with immediacy and liquidity. In fact, you might even come out on the positive end of that small trade. But, if it is a larger order, a bigger fraction of the ADV, it can be your foe because the market can move adversely against you, in the process hurting the quality of your execution. We need to realize that it is not our Grandfather's or Grandmother's market anymore. The exchanges are not public utilities; nowadays they are for-profit businesses. The high-frequency traders are, in effect, the new market makers, in the sense that they are constantly providing liquidity and buying and selling shares on both sides of the trade.

I don't think that anyone would prefer the old system of New York Stock Exchange specialists and NASDAQ market makers and their particular privileges. Because it was discovered that both abused those privileges.[2] Every trader needs to realize that high-frequency trading firms are indeed the new market makers. As such, they are the counterparty to many trades. They can provide liquidity and that immediacy if you demand it. But when they are the counterparty, on many occasions they are trading for a distinct financial purpose. They are trading to make money! You need to be informed and smart about how you deal with that.

I agree with Ari. What is the line between stepping in and making markets and risking capital, versus actually trying to move the market in your favor? When is a high-frequency market maker crossing that line? If there are certain flaws in the system – for example, in the way that quotes and market data are disseminated to high-frequency market makers versus natural buyers and sellers – then those issues need to be addressed.

CHARLES-ALBERT LEHALLE: High-frequency trading is common in both American and European market microstructure. All the same issues are raised on

---

[2] Much attention has been devoted to these controversies in the media and in academic studies. First, NASDAQ market makers were accused in the late 1980s of abusing their privileges by not providing liquidity and two-sided continuous quotes at the time of the 1987 market crash. That led to the introduction of the Small Order Execution System (SOES). More significantly, these same market makers were also accused of colluding to keep bid ask spreads on stock prices artificially wide, a practice characterized by only quoting stocks in even one eight increments (0.2/8, 4/8, 6/8). Later, specialists on the New York Stock Exchanges were accused of "flipping" and "trading for eights" and "interpositioning" themselves unfairly on some orders to the disadvantage of institutional and retail customer orders. These scandals led to a series of market structure reforms.

See, Christie WG, Thompson RB (2006) Wall Street scandals: the curative effects of law and finance. Wash U Law Rev http://lawreview.wustl.edu/inprint/84-7/christiethompson.pdf

See, For Whom the Bell Tolls: The Demise of Exchange Trading Floors and the Growth of ECNs, Page 900. Jerry W. Markam, General Counsel and Director of Compliance, Iowa Grain Company and Daniel J Harty, Professor of Law, Florida International University School of Law at Miami, September 18, 2008. http://www.law.uiowa.edu/documents/jcl/Volume%2033/4/Markhamfinal.pdf

the two different zones. What do we have in common that explains this? Because Reg NMS and MiFID[3] are not that close in scope. The common denominator could be the fragmentation of markets. It has been said before that if you want to break a monopoly, you have to pay a price for that. Put another way, we cannot both curb fragmentation and foster competition at the same time between exchanges or trading platforms without having people building bridges of liquidity between all those pools. That is the price that has to be paid. Let me be clear. When a HFT trader provides liquidity via quotes on an ATS or exchange, and then unwinds its position – simultaneously providing liquidity on the other side of the trade on some other venue – the HFT trader builds what I call a liquidity bridge between the two venues. And this is the friend side of the answer. The foe side is this: To what extent do we agree to pay a price – the fact that a market participant does not have the luxury of a few seconds, or anytime, to wait for a counterparty to respond to this same market participant in fast-moving markets. Where do we draw the line?

Okay, the HFT traders build these bridges to create liquidity. But, how much value do they offer the marketplace? How do they change the market microstructure; how do they try to avoid that and instead put some limits on their activities? Of course, HFT traders can be both friends and foes. To sum up, when I answer questions about high-frequency traders, I always note that there is a price to be paid for fragmentation. It may be a hard price, but we have to pay it if we want competition between trading platforms.

DOREEN MOGAVERO: My trading background is much more human-based than it is in electronic trading. Mine is an odd answer for someone who is really operating in a more human marketplace. I am actually a friend. I like the high-frequency traders and the purpose that they serve. It is very useful in terms of the added liquidity and decreasing spreads this brings.

My bigger question is something that is not particularly related to high-frequency trading. It is related to the overall electronic trading in the markets. In my opinion, we have swung too far towards electronic trading in favor of thinking that humans have little to contribute anymore to this process. However, I would be much more inclined to say that I am a friend of the high-frequency traders and consider them market makers. To that end, I appreciate the liquidity they bring to the market.

The focus more recently has been on high-frequency trading rather than on the overall electronic marketplace. Because the volumes that they – the high-frequency traders – are responsible for today are very, very high. The institutional investor is out of the market to a greater degree than before. I have heard anywhere from 35

[3]Regulation NMS, or National Market System, was enacted by the Securities and Exchange Commission in 2007 to foster competition among US exchanges and individual orders, and to promote fairness in price executions across all exchanges and platforms.

MiFID, the Markets in Financial Instruments Directive was enacted as European Union law on November 1, 2007 to foster competition and investor protection. It harmonizes the regulation of financial services among EU member nations.

percent to 65 percent of the volumes today are related to high-frequency trading.[4] When you become that much of the marketplace you automatically become a focus. I am not so sure that focus is warranted.

The high-frequency traders are no different than any other market makers. Having traded in more manual-oriented markets for years, I can tell you the gaming aspect of electronic markets is not something only high-frequency traders do. As soon as our markets became even slightly more electronic, as soon as you posted a bid in this new environment, there was someone who could then game that bid or offer. That led to much darker markets than we've ever had in the past.[5] Here's my point: The overall structure of the market is a much larger problem than whether high-frequency trading is at the root of the problem or not.[6]

In other words, back when I was trading in a more manual market, as soon as I posted a bid the electronic side of this marketplace also interacted with my order at some stage in the trade cycle. As soon as program trading and electronic trading started away from the NYSE, that is when we began to see much more fragmented markets. And when we moved to decimal pricing, penny trading became a phenomena and a challenge as did these dark markets. So, the issue really is more about market structure and not whether HFT is a problem.

LAWRENCE RYAN: High-frequency trading and electronic trading require a lot of tools, such as DMA, or Direct Market Access, fast trading engines, trading models, such as market making, statistical or event arbitrage models, back testing and profitability analysis. In these particular markets, systems are completing a trade in milliseconds; actually the fastest trading systems complete a trade in microseconds. At these speeds, to achieve further speed improvements, matching and trading engines must be co-located.[7] The way I like to phrase this is, 'we're going back to the future.' Years ago, people convened to improve market efficiencies, but now we co-locate computers to minimize trade latency and volatility. Trading is a social

---

[4]As of writing, TABB Group and other analysts estimate HFT share volume hovering around 50 % of the marketplace. On some individual stocks the market share can rise as high as 70 %, they estimate.

[5]The speaker is referring here to dark markets versus lit markets. Dark markets are, in a sense, functionally opposite to lit markets. In lit markets, prices and other trading data are publicly displayed prior to execution, which is not the case in the anonymity of dark markets.

[6]Richard (Rick) Ketchum Chairman & CEO, FINRA, in testimony May 20, 2010, before the US Congressional Subcommittee on Securities, Insurance, and Investment Committee on Banking, Housing, and Urban Affairs picked up on this theme.

Ketchum, said in part: "A generation ago, the vast majority of activity occurred on the equity market that listed the security. Today, orders are routed to some 50 competing platforms. This complex environment creates opportunities for traders seeking unfair advantage to manipulate markets. How? By exploiting inconsistencies or gaps created when the responsibility of regulatory oversight is divided. Regulatory gaps and splintered oversight make it possible for trading abuses—such as market manipulation, marking the close and front-running customer orders—to be carried out furtively across multiple markets, with a reduced chance of detection." See, http://www.finra.org/Newsroom/Speeches/Ketchum/P121509

[7]This refers to the ability of market participants to gain advantages in speed of trade execution through advanced technology, specifically the "co-location" of their computer servers near stock exchanges. That lowers so-called latency, a critical factor in high-speed trade executions.

phenomenon; our trading models attempt to predict market behavior and trade on those predictions.

HFT's demand for faster markets and higher volumes requires cutting-edge commercial use of computer technology. To handle the required trading speeds and market volumes at minimal volatility requires fine tuning the technology platform across the trading lifecycle. HFT has helped drive the growth of real-time operating systems, faster system bus speeds[8], faster network technology, such as Infiniband[9], and faster middleware technology, such as messaging systems.

But, because traders trade across multiple markets, they also must connect and route orders to those markets, which requires a local and global trading strategy. To attract order flow, markets are creating differentiation not just on speed, but by offering innovative trading algorithms and price structures – such as rebates on order flow. For example, Direct Edge's EDGX market charges higher fees for liquidity takers and provides higher rebate for liquidity providers than their EDGA market.

As we build faster trading systems, achieving even greater speed will require even greater investment. We will reach a limit where we can't build faster systems because we can't send electrons faster than the speed of light. Today, the Singapore Stock Exchange can process an order in less than 90 microseconds; and we have proved in our labs that we can decrease trading speed to less than 20 microseconds. Market venues and participants will need to seek new differentiations as fast trading speeds become the new norm.

GATHERAL: Cameron, friend or foe?

CAMERON SMITH: We have to begin from a basic starting point. Markets need market professionals to provide liquidity. Systems like Liquidnet and Instinet[10] tried to create markets that were for institutions only. That seems to be the trading nirvana. In this way, one institution wants to buy Microsoft, the other institution wants to sell Microsoft. They meet in a trading system and there is no market impact – and so they all sing halleluiah together! Unfortunately, markets that don't have professional traders don't seem to have enough liquidity. They never get enough market share; nor do they get enough transactions.

Our experience has shown that, in a continuous market setting, you need market professionals to bridge those gaps between supply and demand. A high-frequency trader is a professional who uses automation. And there have been professional traders for hundreds of years. We have had specialists and market makers for hundreds of years. Now we have what we call – and I hate the term – high-frequency traders, who have just automated the task of these same professional traders. What is the impact? Well, they certainly do it much better today, more efficiently than it

---

[8] 'Bus' speeds are a measure of speed in computer systems.

[9] This refers to a *switched fabric* communications link employed in *high-performance computing*.

[10] Liquidnet, founded in 2001 by Seth Merrin, is the *electronic* brokerage anonymously facilitating block trading among buy-side institutions. Instinet, launched in 1967 as Institutional Networks Corp., is regarded as an early pioneer in electronic trading for institutional investors in a similar anonymous manner.

has been done before. As for the profit margins, look at the LaBranche filing when they went public.[11] What were they making on a per share basis compared to high-frequency firms? It was exponentially much more than what a high-frequency firm makes today.

The profit margins in our industry have shrunk. What we are now taking out of the market is much fairer and the market is more efficient than in the past. We are providing liquidity to the marketplace without any inherent structural advantages. It has leveled the playing field and at a much lower cost. I see it as a tremendous benefit. And we can also look at the market statistics, the conventional measures.

Professor Schwartz mentioned before that he did see some issues at the open which, I think, has a lot more to do with fragmentation than the automation of professional traders. I'd love to hear more about your study, Bob. We know that institutional trading costs have steadily decreased over the last ten years. We know that individual trading costs have declined. And it seems like volatility is on the decline by every measure.

The SEC hosted a panel on the trading markets a few months back. An official from the investment management company, Vanguard, talked about how transaction costs at Vanguard are down 50 percent over the past several years. He talked about saving for retirement and the cost-effective benefits of investing more for greater long-term returns. In that light, I think the market is incredibly healthy today.

High-frequency trading to me is the equivalent of automating the jobs of market professionals. The markets have improved considerably. And I believe HFT has contributed greatly to that.

GATHERAL: Cameron has made a very strong point. Institutional costs have really come down a lot. Ari, do mutual funds think that their costs have declined?

BURSTEIN: Let's clear up some stuff. There is absolutely no doubt transactional costs have come down for institutional investors. We've always noted that fact in our Comment Letters and I have mentioned it in my speeches – the markets are much better today than they were several years ago for investors. Technology is better, and the buy-side has more tools. We are able to actually do more for ourselves rather than going through trading intermediaries. Indeed, in today's markets we are able to do a better job in preventing leakage, and front running compared with years ago, before the introduction of various reforms and changes. That being said, while explicit costs have gone down for sure, implicit costs have probably gone down too. Is that the result of high-frequency trading? I don't know.

---

[11] Here's how Funding Universe described it: "When LaBranche & Co. issued its prospectus, the public learned how lucrative specialist operations could be. In 1998 the firm – including its recent acquisitions – had a pretax profit margin of 45 percent, compared with, for example, 25 percent for the *financial services* firm of Goldman Sachs & Co. and 12 percent for Merrill Lynch & Co., the world's largest brokerage. In 1998 LaBranche's 36 managing directors received $60.2 million in compensation – an average of $1.7 million each. George M.L. (Michael) LaBranche IV and the other 35 managing directors collectively owned about 70 percent of the firm. LaBranche, president, chairman, and chief executive officer, was also a governor of the New York Stock Exchange."

SMITH: By the way, it is not 'probably.' If you believe the evidence, it is more like 'absolutely.' And I am talking about both explicit and implicit costs.

BURSTEIN: There are a lot of studies on overall costs.[12]

LEHALLE: At Credit Agricole Cheuvreux we published a study earlier this year on volatility in Spain.[13] At the time of this study, Spain had not implemented enough flexibility to cost-effectively allow alternative venues to use the available clearing and settlement channels. That prevented Spain from offering trading in the best type of market environment.

We can compare that with the UK, for instance. We found that there is no evidence of an increase of volatility there because of high-frequency trading activity. Indeed, I don't think that there are studies that statistically prove that volatility has decreased with high-frequency trading activity. In my mind, it may be the reverse. It is one part of implicit costs, call it that. However, there is a cost in high-frequency trading that nobody talks about – that is infrastructure costs. As soon as you insert one high-frequency trader in the market, you increase the entry cost of any intermediary or market participant. Because this participant has to buy more computers, and network devices, etc. And in terms of the global costs of high-frequency trading, the more you generate quotes the more you increase the costs of a lot of intermediaries that have to store and process market data and quotes.

In this instance, HFT does not increase the cost of prop traders because prop traders do not have to do all that data crunching for clients like other traders have to do. Prop traders do not need to explain to clients that they traded properly. After all, these prop traders work for themselves and not for clients. So, it is a very important point to take into account when we think about the efficiency of high-frequency trading. As I said, there is a price to pay for fragmentation, i.e., competition among trading platforms. And this price isn't that low.

MOGAVERO: Maybe the answer is not to depend on an algorithm and for market participants not to constantly imitate one another on an electronic basis. Maybe the answer is for people to actually do more stock picking? In other words, get away from all that high-frequency trading that's mimicking electronic technology. What we are talking about here is an overarching issue of how much electronics is affecting the way we trade.

STEPHEN SAX (FBN Securities) From the Floor: I am the compliance officer for an NYSE member firm.

Whenever there is an imbalance of orders on the floor of the NYSE – whether on the upside or on the downside – the NYSE specialists would add liquidity, as appropriate. If he saw that there was a market imbalance, he would stop trading in the stocks. And that has always been that way since I've been in the business.

---

[12] For example, see this study as evidence of the decline in implicit and explicit trading costs: Bid-Ask Spread: Measuring Trade Execution Costs in Financial Markets, Hendrik Bessembinde, University of Utah, and Kumar Venkatarama, Southern Methodist University, March 2009. http://kvenkataraman.cox.smu.edu/papers/BVEQF.pdf

[13] Navigating Liquidity 4. Market microstructure: a paradigm shift https://www.cheuvreux.com/pdf/Navigating_Liquidity_september2009.pdf, Crédit Agricole Cheuvreux, April 2010.

On May 6 – the day of the Flash Crash – the NYSE floor acted in the same way. When there was an imbalance of orders they stopped trading in securities. Take, for example, Proctor & Gamble. On May 6 it opened up trading on the floor at $60 a share. Then, suddenly, everything went haywire and stocks started dropping in price. The lowest tick price on May 6 for Proctor & Gamble on the NYSE was $57 a share and some pennies. I don't remember the exact number. But, the stock continued to trade elsewhere with actual prints from $57 down to $39 a share. I don't know how many shares traded. And those were prints that actually stood on the books, while the NYSE stopped trading at $57 a share on the floor.[14]

This is a compliance question: We have had conferences on best execution. As we have always been told, it is very hard to determine what best execution really is. But focus on May 6. In my mind I can't recall another time when there had been a similar imbalance like in Proctor & Gamble on the NYSE floor. In the case of Proctor & Gamble, the electronic venues – the electronic broker dealers that have an obligation to obtain best execution – actually sent orders – to various other venues, which still continued to accept those orders. The bottom line is that prints were made at $39 a share and at $40 a share. Who lost the money in those stocks, and what about the obligation of best execution? I don't know how one can justify best execution in this context if it has been a precedent on the floor of the NYSE to stop trading when there is an imbalance of orders.

GATHERAL: I think everybody here on the panel and in the audience agree that there was a failure in the markets that day. The question is, has it been fixed?

SAX: The question is not whether it been fixed. The question is responsibility. The impression was that the market went down $875 billion in value on May 6 and then went back up. They talk about the Flash Crash. But it had nothing to do with what was happening in the world; it had nothing to do with the e-minis; it had nothing to do with whatever.[15] It had to do with the structure of the marketplace.

GATHERAL: Should high-frequency traders have obligations similar to market makers?

MOGAVERO: No.

The question is, did the high frequency traders cause the Flash Crash? That is what we are trying to get at.

SAX: We have high-frequency trading because we have market fragmentation. So the answer is yes. If we didn't have fragmentation, we wouldn't have this excessive amount of high-frequency trading. I watched the CBS *60 Minutes* segment on[16] high-frequency trading. They had NYSE COO Larry Liebowitz on the floor of some

---

[14] P&G stock drops 37 % – not really, David Goldman, *CNNMoney*. May 6, 2010 http://money.cnn.com/2010/05/06/markets/procter_and_gamble_stock/index.htm

[15] In its report on the Flash Crash, the CFTC and SEC report noted a skittish market environment prior to the Crash because of concern about European sovereign debt. However, the report cited a single sell order of 75,000 S&P E-mini contracts traded at the Chicago Mercantile Exchange as the catalyst for the Crash. Media reports identified the mutual fund Waddell & Reed as the source of that sell order, which was valued at approximately $4.1 billion.

[16] See, Extra: How High Frequency Trading Grew. *60 Minutes*, CBS News www.cbsnews.com/video/watch/?id=6945166n

subterranean basement talking about co-locations.[17] That was at the New York Stock Exchange. Then you had another gentleman supposedly talking about high-frequency trading.

My understanding of high-frequency trading is very simple. Things trade in about 40 or 50 different venues. Certain people have access to these venues, to direct access, to direct pipes that not everybody else has. They are basically able to buy and to sell before somebody else buys and sells. Again, high-frequency trading is caused by fragmentation. If you didn't have fragmentation, you wouldn't have as much high-frequency trading.

GATHERAL: I think everybody agrees. But I should do a quick check that fragmentation was at the root of the Flash Crash.

MOGAVERO: I do agree. It was a huge contributor. Not so much that we are fragmented, but that the rules were not the same across the board.

GATHERAL: There is no obligation for people to make markets?

MOGAVERO: Right. And I think that regulation is a big issue.

CALLAHAN: I agree in terms of the very different rules. You do make a very good point. It is easy to criticize the specialists of old. But there is one very good thing that they did – they allowed natural counterparties to find each other in the marketplace. If there was a sell imbalance, they would often stop the market and expose things to the crowd. There was this idea (which is back to the point about price discovery) of let's try to get the natural counterparties together before the specialist steps in to use his or her own capital.

One of the big things complaints the market today is that institutional investors are using 'market maker' capital on every single trade. That's insofar as they are likely trading with high-frequency market makers who are typically standing between the investors and other natural counterparties.

Here's the thing about fragmentation: There are a lot of new exchanges, but there have also been a lot of new ATSs. A lot of these ATSs, like Liquidnet, and BlockCross, are really about helping institutional investors find each other in the marketplace. So, if these investors are trying a dark pool, they might first go to a Liquidnet, and try to find each other before they go and access other markets.

I agree with Cameron that you will never have a perfect market where natural counterparties can always find each other. You do need people to step in and use capital. We need to make sure that the markets are providing facilities to find each other, to find the natural counterparties.

BURSTEIN: A lot of market inefficiencies that we are dealing with now came together to cause May 6. If we are talking fragmentation friend or foe, from an institutional investor's standpoint, I would have to say that it is probably a foe. It is hard to search out liquidity among some 45 – 50 venues. I am not necessarily saying that having just two venues out there is the best way either. Maybe there is some happy medium.

---

[17]This refers to the ability of market participants to gain advantages in the speed of trade executions through advanced technology, specifically the "co-location" of their computer servers near stock exchanges. That lowers so-called latency, a critical factor in high-speed trade executions.

I would like to refocus on some of the questions on high-frequency trading. I am curious to hear from the rest of the panel about canceled orders. Do we need to deal with that? Is a fee or a penalty warranted? [18] Is that a problem for the markets? When do you cross the line to market manipulation? Those are the issues that we are dealing with as institutional investors. I think that is what the regulators are looking at.

GATHERAL: Should high-frequency traders have market making obligations, assuming that is what we call those people who are trading in these venues that are hard to access for ordinary people? Would the circuit breaker fix a May 6 type situation?

LEHALLE: We have to be very careful talking about circuit breakers. If you have a market structure that is inherently unstable, you will not improve the efficiency of this system by imposing hard limits. By triggering circuit breakers at a 10 percent limit – that is, stopping trades outside of a specified price band at this percentage level above and below the average price of the security – does that mean that you are satisfied with moves of, say nine percent? Or, does it mean that next time around you will consider changing the circuit breaker to moves of nine or eight percent?[19]

You've got to change the market design to accommodate more frictions into it. Is demanding obligations of a high-frequency trader a nice way to input more friction in the market? Maybe there are other solutions like regulating the tick size? But if you want to prevent the market microstructure from repeating such events as May 6, you should not impose restrictions like circuit breakers. You really should improve the market's microstructure dynamics. My answer then should be to introduce more frictions in the market.

SMITH: Steve made a comment about how, in his mind, high-frequency trading had to do with fragmentation. They are completely unrelated. Oftentimes, we forget that the US equity market is the only market in the world of its kind. It certainly is the premier market, the most efficient and largest market in the world. Then again, it is not the only market. For instance, there are futures that trade in a centralized fashion on the Chicago Mercantile Exchange (CME). And yet the CME has a large percentage of HFT players. Similarly, if you go to Europe, those markets are much more centralized than our markets. And yet, they also have a high percentage of HFT players. So, we see markets with HFT and still, they have little to no fragmentation. This shows they – HFT and fragmentation – are unrelated concepts.

---

[18] See, Traders May Face Nordic-Style EU Fee for Cancelled Orders, Jim Brunsden, *Bloomberg News* http://www.bloomberg.com/news/2012-03-23/high-frequency-traders-may-face-eu-fees-on-excessive-orders.html

[19] As of writing June 2012, the SEC had approved two proposals to address "extraordinary volatility" in individual stocks and the stock market generally. One is a "limit-up and limit down" proposal. The second updates existing market-wide circuit breakers. Under this proposal, the circuit breakers, when triggered, would halt trading in all exchange-listed securities throughout the US markets. The exchanges and FINRA planned to implement these changes by February 4, 2013. As background, See, SEC Announced Filing of Limit Up-Limit Down Proposal to Address Extraordinary Market Volatility, SEC Press Release, April 5, 2011. http://www.sec.gov/news/press/2011/2011-84.htm

Professional, high-frequency trading bridges the gap between supply and demand. It reduces fragmentation, it does not increase it. Maybe at the edges it allows people to pursue strategies that you were talking about. But, by and large, the vast majority of trading is done using predictive models that bridge these gaps between supply and demand. It does not matter if there are 40 markets or one market for that product.

On the CME, a significant percentage of the trading is done by what we are now calling (for some reason) high-frequency trading. This goes into your market-making obligations question. Once again, look around at the other markets, and you will see that the CME is a great example. They don't have a market-making class there. In Europe none of the major markets have market makers. It was a conscious decision to eliminate the market making here. Because typically, when you give market makers obligations, you are also giving them a benefit. Then we start falling into that world which we just left in the late 90's and early 2000's.

I spent a lot of time on those battles when I was at Island, back in the day when you had a two-tiered market.[20] Certain people may accept having obligations, but they will not do so for no apparent reason. They want to know what's in it for them. If you get a benefit, you get a class of liquidity providers. That limits competition because they have an advantage over everyone else. That means that there is a group of people who have the advantage. People who don't have the advantage can't compete with them and it reduces liquidity. Ironically, I think that if you had market-maker obligations, you would actually reduce liquidity. Yet people are saying we need market-making obligations to reduce the chance of a Flash Crash again. We saw, however, that the CME preformed well during the Flash Crash. They just had the circuit breaker and no market maker obligations. I don't think it was a coincidence that, at the bottom of the market at the CME on May 6, the market paused for a mere five seconds before coming right back up.

The US equity market, globally, is the only market that I know of that doesn't have a market-wide style circuit breaker.[21] So, it mystifies me when people want to point to the lack of a market-making obligation as a cause of the Flash Crash when several markets in the world clearly contradict this view. Common sense shows that one factor, the lack of this circuit breaker, is correlated with the actual occurrence of a Flash Crash.

BURSTEIN: I'd like to make a point about market makers. There have been a lot of high-frequency trading firms saying that we need more responsibilities on

[20]Cameron Smith was general counsel at Island ECN from 1999 to 2002. He is referring here to the market structure that prevailed prior to the introduction of reforms such as the 1997 order handling rules. His argument is that NASDAQ market makers and NYSE specialists had an unfair access to stock pricing and execution services over retail investors. Subsequently, limit order protection rules, for example, helped to "level the playing field" for retail investors.

[21]Since the Flash Crash, measures were adopted to introduce such a market-wide mechanism. See, Regulators Adopt Tools to Prevent Another Flash Crash, Ben Protess, *New York Times*, June1, 2012, http://dealbook.nytimes.com/2012/06/01/regulators-adopt-new-tools-to-prevent-another-flash-crash/

certain market maker participants. Let's be realistic. If another May 6 occurs, whatever the market maker responsibilities may have been, they would not have stopped a Flash Crash. No one is going to get in front of a run-away train. I think we on the buy-side realize that. Cameron touched on this. You need to look at the overall impact on the markets and on market structure. If you give the benefits to more market participants, what will come out of that? That needs to be thrown into the scenario as well.

MOGAVERO: More often than not, obligations are not profitable. As a trader with obligations you are typically on the contra, or opposite side of a market trend. In other words, when you have a significantly meaningful obligation, you are forced to buy stock in the absence of buyers, and to sell stock in the absence of sellers. That is not really the problem we are discussing here. We are trying to figure out if high-frequency trading in any way disadvantages the rest of the trading community. In this context, you look at factors such as co-location and gaming.[22] Gaming is an electronic issue, not a high-frequency issue. Co-location is something similar. If market participants feel they can't pay for it, they are at a geographic and trading disadvantage to those participants who can pay for it.

Can the regulators level the playing field across the board? Different pockets of traders have different advantages in the marketplace. That includes internalized order flow that I am unable to get to when I am trying to trade for my client because this order flow is somewhere else; or it is electronically jammed in some pipe because of a million cancellations a second! There is a disadvantage no matter where you turn to, and that disadvantage is someone else's advantage.

The bigger question is, why haven't the regulators addressed the market on that level rather than continuing to add layers and layers of rules on top of a basic surface that is not working?

GATHERAL: Speed up the consolidated feed of market data. This is a very practical suggestion. What do people think about that? One of the disadvantages that people at large firms incur is with the consolidated feeds. The delivery is very slow at larger firms compared to the direct feeds that high-frequency traders take advantage of.

MOGAVERO: But, there is no standardization of technology across the board for anyone. Maybe that is an issue that should be looked into?

GATHERAL: Everybody knows what high-frequency traders do. They have some model for predicting order flow or predicting price movement. When does that become manipulation? I am paraphrasing Ari's question. You predict the price movement, or you predict the order flow that you trade against. When is that gaming? When is gaming manipulation? Ari?

---

[22] According to critics, high-frequency trading permits gamers to flush out large orders by electronically 'pinging' small market orders to buy and sell. In this way, these gamers may unearth a larger order when several small orders are filled.

BURSTEIN: It is a grey area. FINRA has addressed some cases. For example, there was the case of Trillium Brokerage Services though it was not necessarily related to high-frequency trading.[23] The regulators are looking at what is happening. I am not saying this is market manipulation or crossing the line, but these things certainly needs to be examined. If you put orders into a market and withdraw them immediately just to draw other market participants in, or if you have no intention of executing an order, or else you induce others to change their quotes. These are problems.

Everybody is trying to figure out what everybody else is doing. If you are doing high-frequency trading, we don't have a problem with that per se as long as you are executing orders. But if you are throwing in 5,000 quotes a second and you are not executing anything – in effect, you are quote stuffing. Is that manipulative?[24] We are waiting for the regulators to see about this. I don't think there is a clear answer.

GATHERAL: Doreen, was there gaming since the beginning of the world?

MOGAVERO: You've got to prove intent. If a trader of any kind puts an order in the marketplace, the intent is to have that order executed. If they have decided that the time frame in which they are willing to take the risk with their money is shorter and shorter, I see that as a market-making job, providing liquidity or not providing liquidity. I also don't see why anyone should be able to enter an order and then take it back with extreme speed.

GATHERAL: Should we make people leave their orders in for 500 milliseconds because it levels the playing field?

LEHALLE: What is gaming? We can answer what is at the heart of this question without specifically answering the question itself. Before knowing what gaming is and is not, we need to give regulators the ability to investigate this. So they will need to record all that activity and perform data crunching in order to make decisions. I have had a lot of discussions about this with the European regulators. As you may not know, Europe is far more fragmented than the US. Because of that, it is far more difficult for regulators to track gaming in Europe. High-frequency traders, by inserting more and more quotes, are increasing the investigation costs of regulators. We have got to think about that. The regulators simply have to buy more computers and build more sophisticated software and be able to resynchronize heterogeneous data coming from all available trading venues.

---

[23] In September 2010, the Financial Industry Regulatory Authority censured and fined Trillium Brokerage Services LLC $1 million and also fined and suspended 11 of its employees in relation to engaging an "illicit high-frequency trading strategy and related supervisory failures" to gain an advantage. Trillium was accused of entering "numerous" layered, market-moving orders that triggered selling or buying interest in certain stocks. By submitting these orders, according to FINRA, Trillium "created a false appearance of buy- or sell-side pressure." In that way, FINRA said Trillium gained a superior price advantages that would not have been possible to them in "46,000 instances."

[24] Some analysts would regard the Trillium episode as a form of quote stuffing, the practice of submitting an excessive amount of larger orders to buy or sell stocks in fractions of a second and then canceling the orders almost immediately.

It goes back to the argument of an increase in the technological costs for everyone except the prop traders. We've got to think that way about how to use high-frequency trading properly to improve market efficiency. It can be done. To answer your question more directly, we can do this by increasing the friction in the markets. For instance, by making people pay for some cancellations of orders; or maybe by demanding that orders stay at least x- milliseconds in the market, or maybe by just increasing the tick size. Any friction that can be put in the market will decrease the high-frequency activity of participants. I think that this is the proper way to control the activity of high-frequency trading. Then the regulators have to find the proper limits to put on these frictions.

GATHERAL: I can tell from Cameron's face that he is against friction.

SMITH: Increasing friction is an oblique way of saying let's increase trading costs! I guess I don't understand why we would want to intentionally increase trading costs unless we could identify the specific problem that it would solve. The 'problem' hasn't been identified. Yet it has been said that there is too much trading by professional traders who use automation, and these professionals have been called high-frequency traders. Is this somehow degrading market quality? The evidence points the other way. And if you could somehow slow it down, would that improve market quality? No way. There are a lot of links in that chain that are really interesting and should be explored. All I know is that market microstructure is very fragile. To arrive at that conclusion without evidence, and then to try and implement policies that can have all kinds of consequences, is dangerous.

Cancellations are an interesting issue. Consider somebody who has a trading strategy with a 90 percent cancellation rate. That may seem high to someone who is not privy to the nature of automated trading. On the other side of the coin, these automated trading firms with high cancellation rates are the same firms that account for a significant percentage of the volume. You have this self-contradictory viewpoint where people are saying on the one hand, that it is phantom liquidity if they are putting up all these orders and canceling them, and if I can't interact with them. On the other hand, these same critics would agree that high-frequency traders account for 50 – 60 percent of the market. The obvious question is if nobody can interact with these quotes, then how is it that HFT is 60 percent of the market? Clearly some people are able to interact with HFT, and liquidity is an important part of the market.

RYAN: But volume doesn't equal stable liquidity. A high-frequency trader may exit the market or not supply deep inventory, meaning the HFT trader could choose not to offer substantial liquidity in the marketplace.

SMITH: That is an interesting statement. I am not saying it is wrong, but rather that we should talk about it.

GATHERAL: A question from the audience.

JOE ROSEN (RKA Inc.) From the Floor: I am a free-market capitalist. I am not some anti-technology Luddite. I am not a Communist. To some extent it seems to me that we are dancing around the issue and dealing with the symptoms rather than the disease. I would venture to say – and it seems that everyone agrees with this – that there is too much fragmentation. What is the right number of ATSs and market venues? Should there be only one trading venue? There are now dozens of ATSs and exchanges. Is that the perfect number or not? I don't know. Many people agree that there are too many places to trade.

Let me say something about monopolies. They are a bad thing. I am not suggesting that in the equity execution business there should only be one place. Of course, the DTTC[25] is a natural monopoly, and that makes a lot of sense. That's a separate matter.

So, I ask this question: Do we have too much fragmentation? I am not saying the SEC should come in and say the magic number is X number of market venues.

MOGAVERO: I don't think that anybody is adverse to competition. I am certainly not adverse to electronics. In fact, during the whole Reg NMS debate, I was one of the NYSE floor directors who embraced technology. An integration of the two – manual markets and technology-driven markets – is an absolutely perfect marriage. I do not think that we are adverse to competition at all. In fact, our company – Mogavero, Lee & Company – embraces and likes it. The question we have here is whether a high-frequency trader is different than any other trader. I would like that question to be answered. To me, it seems as though people want a sub set of rules for high-frequency traders and not for other traders.

BURSTEIN: Doreen, I agree with you. We should not focus on high-frequency traders; we should focus on the practices. I don't care who is canceling the orders, whether it is high frequency traders, hedge funds, or whoever it might be. We just haven't identified the benefit of a huge canceled order rate, and what that brings to the market.

MOGAVERO: There are many advantages and disadvantages across the board. The problem needs to be addressed on many different levels. The problem is not just unique to high-frequency trading.

GATHERAL: Everyone agrees that we should not pick out just high-frequency traders. Rules should be for everyone. As Cameron has been pointing out, the term is impossible to define. Kevin, do you want to say something in support of fragmentation?

CALLAHAN: Does the world need another dark crossing pool? Probably not. Does it need an exchange that operates like all other exchanges? Probably not. The question about fragmentation really becomes a question about innovation and competition.

Do traders and investors both need new ways to trade? Absolutely. The high-frequency trading world has had a five-year head start on other market participants who need to catch up with them In any event, some of these other market participants are getting smarter about the HFT tools. They are getting smarter about how they operate, and they are looking for new ways to tackle problems. Yet we need be careful. We need to find out if investors and traders support more competition, if they want more choice or less.

BERNARD DONEFER (Baruch College) From the Floor: I don't like the idea of calling it high-frequency trading. I think that is the first mistake. In low-latency, high-frequency trading, a number of strategies are used. We have those who are

---

[25] The Depository Trust & Clearing Corporation.

market makers and who make their money with a passive strategy. They may also make money by rebate collection. We have another group who are quant traders who use various mathematical models in pairs trading. There is a third group – we will call these the bad actors, the people who may be doing things that are causing problems in the market.

Is "quote stuffing" a new term to describe market makers canceling and replacing orders? Are they trying to manipulate the market? We have to separate these things out and not just look at the cancel rates. We have to say, what were the purposes of the cancel rates? As long as we call it high-frequency trading, everybody is somehow tarred with the one brush. We lose the nuance that we need to solve the problems we have described today.

PROFESSOR ROBERT SCHWARTZ: I would like to step outside the title of the session on high-frequency trading and circle back to the basic theme of the conference, which is market quality, and assessing market quality. I pay a lot of attention myself to the quality of price discovery and how to measure it. As I said in my opening remarks, you can't do that directly. I am inferring it from the volatility in the market.

You have seen some of my findings. At this point, I would like to get a sense from this panel of what your view is on the quality of price discovery in this new environment? Is it better, is it sharper, or is it nosier?

LAHALLE: What is quite new is this: If we rely on people providing liquidity in high- frequency trading who are also hedging, then maybe we can have liquidity available in the market when the position is easy to hedge. All liquidity providers who are also high- frequency traders will only provide liquidity when it is compatible with the main ETFs or main market factors that are easy to hedge. There is a study by Boyan Jovanic and Albert Menkveld. Titled "Middlemen in Limit-Order Markets[26]". Their findings were in that direction.

CALLAHAN: I would like to share one quick story. I was talking to a sell-side trader last week who said, "I have one side of a trade and I know there is another broker who had the other side of the trade. In the old days, we would meet on the Midwest Stock Exchange and we would put up a block. Now we are both trading against each other all day long, and there are these high-frequency traders in the middle taking a piece." I return to Bob Schwartz's question, it is an example of how price discovery has gotten a little noisier.

MOGAVERO: Clearly the market has become more fragmented. It is more difficult for traders to find each other. It is darker. A lot of information is not publicly available because of dark pools and the likes of internalization. The fragmentation, the darkness in the market, and the access to liquidity, are issues that need to be addressed. There are huge private pools of liquidity. There is a huge proportion of liquidity in the market that is controlled by a small group of firms through internalization and because of market fragmentation. That is not a positive development.

GATHERAL: Great final comment.

[26] Middlemen in Limit-Order Markets, Boyan Jovanovic, New York University, Department of Economics and Albert J. Menkveld, VU University Amsterdam, Tinbergen Institute, October 24, 2011. http://www.amf-france.org/documents/general/9414_1.pdf

Chapter 2
Mid-Day Address

Reto Francioni, *CEO, Deutsche Börse AG*

The importance of improving and preserving the quality of our global financial markets has been underlined by recent events – the turbulence in our markets that triggered the so-called Flash Crash in May 2010.[1] We may not have seen the last of it. And while in recent months the volatility in our markets is at the core of worldwide discussions among regulators, politicians, media, and the public, managing volatility has always, from their inception, been the central issue for exchange organizations. This year the Frankfurt Stock Exchange celebrated its 425th anniversary. Some issues like the aforementioned, it seems, never run out of fashion. That's even if there are phases in which they manifest a special sense of urgency. And right now we are in the middle of such a phase.

This said, I would like to propose three major theses today. My first and central thesis is that financial markets are currently entering a new landscape. The major feature of this new landscape is a trend towards re-regulation which is replacing three decades of de-regulation.

Second, one of the key developments that has a strong influence on exchange functionalities, trading technology, and the safety and integrity of markets, is high-frequency trading, or HFT. Algorithmic trading, in general, is related to this development. I believe that the case against HFT is generally overstated. From an exchange point of view, HFT poses primarily a technical and functional challenge.

Third, exchanges' market design is not only meant to make markets more efficient, but also to increase their safety and integrity. One important design feature

---

The views expressed by the speaker reflect prevailing market conditions at the time of the conference.

[1] As described elsewhere in this book, the Flash Crash was characterized by a sudden fall in prices in US exchange-listed stocks, followed immediately by a recovery seemingly unrelated to any change in market fundamentals by some accounts; cf. Securities and Exchange Commission and Commodity Futures Trading Commission: Findings Regarding the Market Events of May 6, 2010. Joint report, 30 September 2010. Available at: http://www.sec.gov/news/studies/2010/marketevents-report.pdf

R.A. Schwartz et al. (eds.), *The Quality of Our Financial Markets: Taking Stock of Where We Stand*, Zicklin School of Business Financial Markets Series,
DOI 10.1007/978-1-4614-5592-9_2,

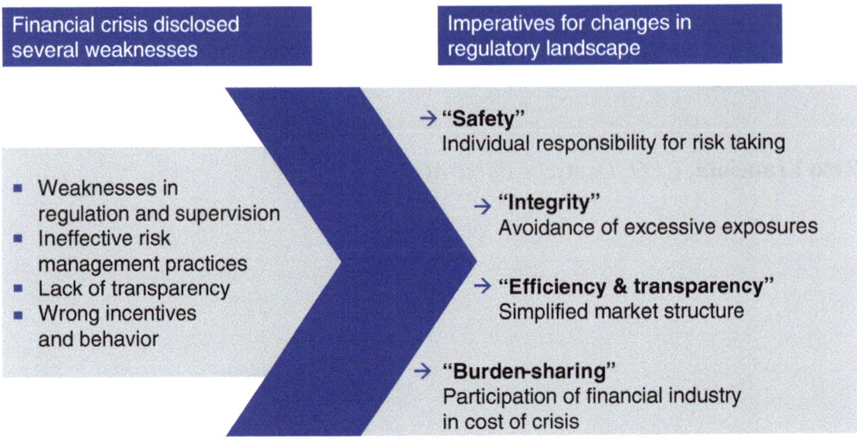

Exhibit 2.1 Financial crisis makes regulators / politicians rethink regulatory landscape

is a functionality called "volatility interruption." In fact, I covered this two years ago at this very conference. Since then it has gained a new significance, especially in the aftermath of the Flash Crash on May 6.

New Landscape: Re-regulation, Safety and Integrity

As I said, the new landscape of financial markets worldwide is, among other things, characterized by a wave of re-regulation. Hopefully that is effective regulation, not over-regulation. As shown in Exhibit 2.1, this new landscape follows four principles. First: Safety, by increasing individual responsibility for risk-taking. Second: Integrity, by avoiding excessive exposure. Third: Efficiency and transparency, by simplifying market structures. And fourth: Burden-sharing, by making the financial industry participate in the cost of coping with the consequences of the financial crisis, and of preventing future crises.

By doing so, regulators and policy makers are trying to address weaknesses in regulation and supervision, ineffective risk management practices, lack of transparency, as well as problematic incentives and behavior. The target of regulation is *not* the exchange sector, which worked perfectly well amid the financial hurricane. Rather, the target is the financial sector in general, particularly banks. Nevertheless, exchanges will still be heavily affected.

This has an ethical side as well. As the *New York Times* columnist Thomas Friedman recently put it, "A larger problem we have not faced honestly as we have dug out of this recession: We had a values breakdown – a national epidemic of get-rich-quickism and something-for-nothingism. … In a flat world where everyone has access to everything, values matter more than ever."[2]

Not that Europe would be exempt from this critique. Like it or not, what we need in today's financial sector (be it in America, be it in Europe, or indeed globally) is nothing less than a paradigm shift: in terms of regulation on the one hand, and in terms of the underlying values on the other hand.

For us as market organizers, and also for market participants, this new landscape is much more complex than the one that we have grown used to during the past ten years. Paradoxically, re-regulation is not accompanied by a *de*crease in competition (that is usually associated with tightening regulation), but by an *in*crease in competition in a shrinking market. The unique selling proposition for market organizers in this new landscape is no longer technology. It is risk management services that help customers to fulfill new regulatory demands, and that make the underlying financial system safer. As a consequence, risk management moves into the focus of exchange activities.

A new paradigm that could be suitable for this new era should include a strong state regulator, and a clear set of rules and standards establishing safety and integrity, combined with functioning markets. These rules and standards ultimately need to be implemented at a global scale to be effective. However, setting rules and standards does not mean intervening in the actual corporate governance of business plans. On the contrary, it means setting a reliable framework that makes markets work in the way the masterminds of economic wisdom saw it. Adam Smith, Walter Eucken, or Friedrich von Hayek, conceptualized it as an instrument for maximising social welfare, for limiting the concentration of power, or for discovering new products and processes. In the present context, the rebalancing of this framework should be governed by an increased concern for safety and integrity, translating into measures for improving risk-mitigation and transparency.

Let me point out two examples of current European policy initiatives within the new paradigm with reference to Exhibit 2.2: First, the regulation of OTC derivatives and, second, equity market structure.

The first initiative regarding OTC derivatives aims at increasing the safety and integrity of markets. Gary Gensler, Chairman of the US derivatives regulator, the Commodity Futures Trading Commission, said earlier this year at the Council on Foreign Relations here in New York, referring to the 2009 market turbulence: "I believe that the over-the-counter derivatives were at the heart of the crisis." A lack of price transparency and a lack of central counterparty clearing, he continued, "leaves significant risk in the system, risk that a year ago was borne by the taxpayers in the form of the largest financial bailout in history …. It is time to change the way these markets function and the way they are regulated to benefit the public and to protect the American taxpayers."[3]

---

[2] *New York Times*, 11 September 2010.

[3] Quoted in *Futures and Options Intelligence*, 8 January 2010, p. 3.

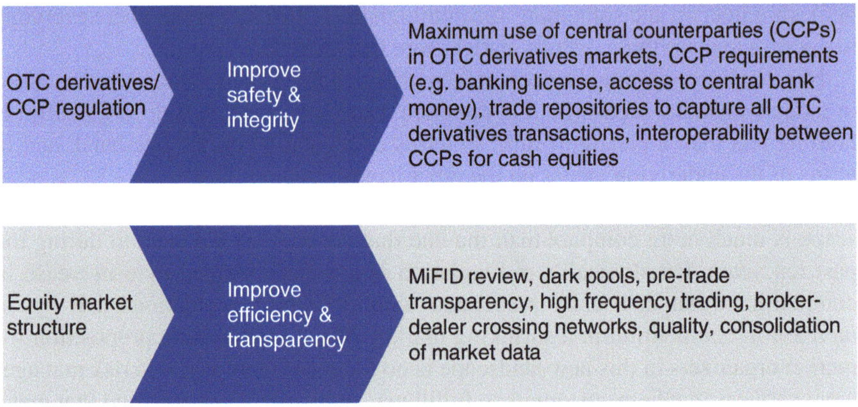

Exhibit 2.2 Core policy initiatives underway: OTC central counterparty

Meanwhile, US legislators have responded, in part via the Dodd-Frank Act[4], although much of the effectiveness of this law regarding OTC derivatives regulation will now depend on the nitty-gritty of definitions left open in the Act that now have to be worked out by the competent authorities. In Europe, a comparable regulation is still in the process of being defined – under the ominous nickname, EMIR ("European Market Infrastructure Regulation") or, more formally: "Financial markets: OTC derivatives, central counterparties and trade repositories."[5]

The proposal makes three very important points: First, it demands a transmission of OTC derivatives trading, wherever possible, to organized markets like exchanges; second, it argues in favour of extending the use of central counterparties to mitigate counterparty risk from exchanges to further sections of the OTC derivatives market; and third, it proposes the introduction of a so-called trade repository (i.e., a database to which all OTC derivatives trades are reported). All three points can only be welcomed from the perspective of safety and integrity, because they introduce important mechanisms for risk mitigation and increased transparency.

This is not the place to indulge in technical details. Let me therefore make just two important points for assessing and further developing the current proposal. The first one concerns the importance of neutrality. Services and functions, such as those provided by central counterparties (CCPs)[6] for the derivatives market, need to be supplied by independent and neutral providers. If risk takers are also burdened with CCP governance, they will be led into a potential conflict of interests between formulating strict rules for risk mitigation on the one hand, and having to bear the cost

---

[4] Summary of Act signed in law by President Obama July 21, 2010, cf. http://banking.senate.gov/public/_files/070110_Dodd_Frank_Wall_Street_Reform_comprehensive_summary_Final.pdf' Full Act, cf., http://www.sec.gov/about/laws/wallstreetreform-cpa.pdf

[5] Cf. http://ec.europa.eu/internal_market/financial-markets/derivatives

[6] Post-trade service providers acting as seller to every buyer and buyer to every seller on derivatives and securities markets. By collecting collateral from market participants in proportion to their risk positions, they effectively insure their trading partners against counterparty risk.

of these rules on the other hand. Because governments will inevitably continue to play the role of the lender of last resort, in the presence of such moral hazard, an arrangement like this would provide strong incentives for suboptimal investing in risk management provisions. It would thus be incompatible with ensuring the safety and integrity of markets.

My second point: When discussing OTC derivatives clearing, we are not talking about an "all or none" alternative. On the contrary, what is needed are market-led initiatives aimed at a CCP clearing of derivatives that has a sufficient degree of standardization. Non-standard derivatives are suitable for neither exchange trading nor for automated clearing. And while I support the greatest possible use of standardized derivatives I, of course, acknowledge that derivatives tailor-made for special needs do play an important role for the economy. Therefore, I believe that an appropriate segmentation of derivatives should be introduced according to their degree of standardization and their suitability for clearing.

Deutsche Börse's CCP is Eurex Clearing.[7] The ongoing procedures and multiple layers of risk protection that are, for instance, in place at Eurex Clearing, helped us in 2008 to successfully wind down all positions involving Lehman Brothers in an orderly and timely manner. Just to remind you, during this process, all risks were covered permanently by sufficient collateral.

The principle behind CCPs is simple: CCPs act as the counterparty to all trading participants, i.e., as buyer to each seller, and as seller to each buyer. By so doing, they effectively insure participants against the risk of counterparty failure. CCPs like Eurex Clearing contribute to risk mitigation in three ways:

- First, they reduce the clearing volume by multilateral netting. In addition, we have installed risk monitoring systems at the customer-level and supply our customers with information on their current risk-level in real-time. Thus we have all the information available online that is necessary for intervening in possible future crisis scenarios at the earliest possible moment.
- Second, we have multiple lines of defence in place in the case a counterparty is unable to pay or deliver. There is a complete cascade of liability to protect our customers from counterparty risk.
- Third, CCPs include a guarantee fund to which all trading participants contribute.

To sum up: Eurex Clearing manages not only counterparty risk but, by monitoring all counterparty risk in real time, it also helps our customers to manage market risk.

Let me now come to the second policy initiative: the European Markets in Financial Instruments Directive (MiFID)[8] with the dual aim of improving the efficiency and transparency of the equity market structure. When introducing MiFID

[7] A subsidiary of Eurex, which in turn is the Deutsche Börse subsidiary operating the derivatives market; cf. http://www.eurexclearing.com

[8] EU directive regulating trading in financial instruments; cf.http://ec.europa.eu/internal_market/securities/isd/mifid_en.htm

three years ago, EU legislators, as well as the EU national governments as represented in the EU Economic and Financial Affairs Council (Ecofin), intended to increase competition between trading venues in order to drive down explicit trading costs. At the same time, pre- and post-trade transparency standards were put in place. That was in order to prevent increased fragmentation from endangering the price discovery function of regulated financial markets and from undermining market integrity that would set in motion a downward spiral for market standards. Ultimately, this sub-set of objectives was meant to benefit investors and companies by driving down capital costs and thus increasing the economic competitiveness of the EU. Currently, MiFID is under review by the European Parliament, the European Commission, and European member states.

MiFID certainly has increased the competition of trading platforms. But it has failed its objective of equally improving market transparency and, even more importantly, investor protection. The estimate of the Federation of European Securities Exchanges on the distribution of the trading volume in Europe is that 40% of share-trading in Europe takes place outside organized markets.

We know even less about the structure of these off-exchange turnovers, i.e., how they are distributed across fixed price transactions, "dark pools," systematic internalizers, etc., and even less about how they have changed during the past two years. At the same time, it is evident that stock exchange business is becoming increasingly pan-European. For example, around 70% of the turnover in shares at Deutsche Börse is carried out by market participants from Europe outside Germany. The *good* news about this is that Europe has already made much greater progress in the capital markets than is often claimed. The *bad* news is that MiFID does not do enough to make the European capital markets safer and more consistent, but instead they have become more opaque – at least up to now.

A recent academic study by Frankfurt University Economics Professor Peter Gomber and others[9] came to another relevant conclusion: The chief justification for using non-organized markets is the ability to carry out very large trades while avoiding adverse market impact. However, as much as 40% of transactions[10] involved trades with an average size of less than €7,500 only. To quote my colleague Roland Bellegarde from Deutsche Börse's competitor, NYSE Euronext: "These trades do not need confidentiality and do not need protection [of an OTC structure]. They have nothing to do with preventing market impact. These transactions do not channel market information nor do they have any market impact; there is absolutely no reason for them to remain confidential. [They] are never going to contribute to price formation."[11]

[9] Gomber P, Pierron A (2010) MiFID – Spirit and reality of a European financial markets directive Frankfurt am Main, Goethe University/Celent, Research Report, September; available at: http://www.wiiw.de/publikationen/MiFIDSpiritandRealityofaEurop3995.pdf

[10] Not order book volume, but number of transactions.

[11] Grant J (2010) Euronext calls for OTC trade threshold. FT.com, 20 Sept, 19:33.

High Frequency Trading and Market Safety

In the public debate, High Frequency Trading (HFT) is often associated with increasing volatility. It is generally regarded with a sense of unease, as if it is a kind of victory in an epic war between machines and human beings. This clearly also reflects the worries of the people on the street after the financial crisis. I would like to take some of the emotion out of the debate and point out some positive contributions HFT makes to market quality. That is while taking the concerns in terms of the safety and integrity of markets very seriously as well.

Electronic trading is nothing new in the securities industry. In 2009, more than 98% of exchange trading in the 30 most liquid German shares included in the DAX index, measured by order book volume, took place on Deutsche Börse's electronic cash market trading system, Xetra.[12] We have become used to the idea of our savings being stored safely in electronic vaults. We routinely transfer money, buy shares, and even subscribe to insurance contracts online. And so we tend to accept it as a natural fact that our securities orders are dealt with, not by human servants, but by electronic servers.

However, what still requires some getting used to is that, in recent years, on securities markets worldwide, orders are not only matched, cleared and settled by computers. They are also increasingly being *generated* by computers. On Xetra, for example, more than 40% of transaction volume was generated electronically in 2009. That's nearly three times as much as the 15% it had taken up in 2003.

Exhibit 2.3 shows the sheer technological challenge this shift in trading patterns means for our electronic trading system, Xetra. While system latency has drastically decreased to keep up with the rising speed of trading, the number of transactions has vastly increased as well. With an annual compound growth rate of more than 30% between 2002 and 2010, we have seen a more than 10-fold increase in transaction numbers and a more than 25-fold increase in speed, or a corresponding decrease in "latency," to use the technical term. On our backbone line to London, for instance, we have reached speeds for one-way data transmissions of less than 5 milliseconds.

Algo trading exists in various forms, each corresponding to a specific type of trading strategy that has been made possible by technological sophistication. First, there are high-frequency traders who carry arbitrage down to miniscule differences between prices traded on different venues and at different points of time; they do so at speeds far faster than the blink of an eyelid. Second, there are electronic liquidity providers who perform the function of market makers on the basis of new electronic technologies. And third, there are brokers who use computers to split large orders up into many small ones, thus avoiding harmful market impact; the strategy is known as "slice and dice."

Algo trading is not entirely uncontroversial, at least among some policy makers and financial regulators (and neither, naturally, among their slower competitors in

---

[12] Deutsche Börse's electronic regulated market for securities; cf. http://xetra.com

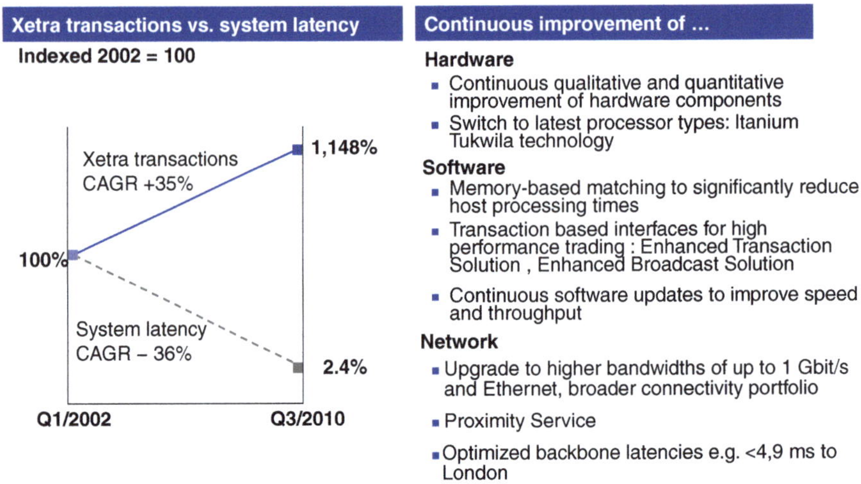

Exhibit 2.3 Algorithmic trading on Xetra: more than 10-fold increase in transaction numbers and more than 25-fold increase in speed

the banking sector). At times, for example, the claim is made that algo traders, by buying when markets go up, and selling when they go down, reinforced market volatility. However, I believe that there are also good arguments supporting quite the contrary – in spite of accusations made in the context of the so-called "Flash Crash" on May 6.

Researchers from the University of California Berkeley, Columbia Business School, and the University of Amsterdam, in an article published in the *Journal of Finance*, carried out an econometric study based on NYSE data. They arrive at the conclusion: "Algorithmic trading lowers the costs of trading and increases the informativeness of quotes." And they raise a further point which is especially relevant in the face of growing fears of a credit squeeze for the real economy. They write, "This could ultimately reduce the cost of capital for firms."[13]

I have nothing to add to this judgement – except my wish that such voices are heard in the regulatory discussion currently led in the US and in Europe. Nevertheless, I remind us all never to forget that we cannot expect to live an undistorted life in a theoretically perfect exchange world. We must accept that societies have fears about the financial markets. We are part of these societies. And it is our duty to explain what we do and to accept that societies need to make sure that they have things under control.

[13] Hendershott T, Jones CM, Menkveld AJ (2010) Does algorithmic trading improve liquidity? J Finance 66:1–33; available at http://papers.ssrn.com/sol3/papers.cfm?abstract_id=1100635#

I have two comments on the Flash Crash. First, it should not be forgotten that the SEC has also pointed out the role of internalization firms in the Flash Crash. To quote the SEC report: "Many internalizers of retail order flow stopped executing as principal for their customers that afternoon, and instead sent orders to the exchanges, putting further pressure on the liquidity that remained in those venues."

To me, this seems like another piece of evidence that when times get tough, exchanges are used as safe havens for order execution. At the same time, it demonstrates the fragility of a market structure that splits up order execution over too wide an array of trading platforms that do not operate on a level playing field in terms of regulation. I am not arguing in favour of transferring all trading to regulated markets or exchanges. However, if we are willing to introduce competition between markets, then these markets need to operate on the same transparency levels. If not, we undermine the safe and orderly functioning of price discovery. I believe that the Flash Crash has shown very drastically the practical importance of a seemingly abstract concept such as "price discovery."

Second, a quote from the *Financial Times Deutschland*: "The result of [the SEC's] analysis of the Flash Crash suggests that the functioning of the entire exchange trading in the US needs to be improved. The market is fragmented – there are more than 30 active platforms. Regulators have already admitted that the connections and the communication between the large number of trading platforms had worsened the problem."[14] You are all in a better position to judge whether there is some truth in this or not. I will leave it uncommented – except to make one final point: namely, we at Deutsche Börse have for many years introduced a safeguard to protect markets against excessive volatility at the micro level. I will discuss this next.

How to Handle Volatility

One common approach taken by exchanges and imposed by regulators in order to deal with volatility has been the introduction of circuit breakers.[15] There are three types of circuit breakers: price limits circuit breakers, which allow trading only within a certain price corridor; firm-specific trading halts that apply to single stocks only; and market-wide trading interruptions.

When designing Deutsche Börse's electronic trading system, Xetra, we focused on what we call "volatility interruptions." As shown in Exhibit 2.4 volatility interruptions on Xetra combine price limits not with trading halts, but with a switch in the trading form of an individual instrument from continuous trading into call auction mode.

[14] FTD online, 1.10.2010, 10:51, Christine Mai, Frankfurt: US-Aufseher lösen Rätsel um "Flash Crash".

[15] Mechanisms that automatically interrupt trading in situations of high volatility.

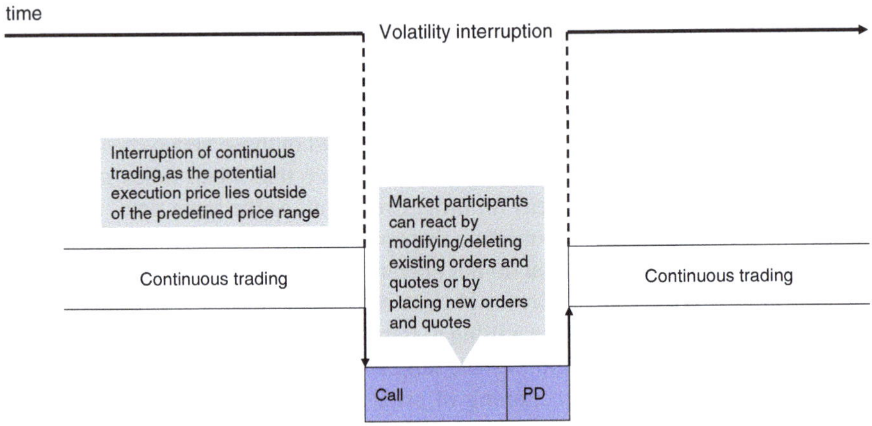

Exhibit 2.4 Increasing market safety at the micro level: volatility interruption during continuous trading

The interruption of continuous trading is triggered when a new price for a stock would be outside a pre-defined static price range. That is based on the last paid price, combined with historical volatility, and also combined with a dynamic price range that differs for each individual stock. As a consequence, the individual overall price range is unknown to market participants. Leaving the limit unknown precludes the possibility of a willingly introduced interruption of continuous trading for tactical reasons. The mechanism works like this. When the upper or lower price limit is potentially crossed, all market participants are informed, and a call auction is started with the order-book situation at that point in time.

The auction concentrates liquidity, and the message that is sent to all market participants attracts further liquidity. This increase in liquidity in and of itself improves the price discovery process. If strong price deviations persist after the auction, our market supervision desks contact the traders who have caused them. In addition, the exchange management may also stop trading in individual shares if major price-relevant news is in the offing.

In short, volatility interruptions:

- Work on a stock by stock basis
- Do not interrupt the price discovery process
- Use a static and a dynamic price range

Volatility interruptions are aimed especially at less liquid shares. They are, however, valid for all shares, including our most liquid shares in the DAX™ 30. On Xetra, we trade as many as 12,000 different financial instruments. As you can imagine, volatility interruptions are therefore quite frequent: On a normal trading day, we handle between 600 and 700 of them, mostly in illiquid shares. In our 30 most liquid DAX™ shares, we normally have less than ten volatility interruptions per trading day for all shares taken together. On exceptional trading days, the number can, however, also reach more than 100. I think this underlines the importance of the micro-management of the trading process practised by exchanges for the safety of their markets.

On the whole, volatility interruptions play an essential role in our efforts to guarantee smooth and orderly price discovery. We believe that they are an effective way of dealing with situations of heightened volatility. That is by allowing price discovery always to continue and, at the same time, by avoiding a vicious circle of ever increasing price movements.

This also means that, as usual, index calculation goes on permanently during trading hours. And it implies that derivatives trading based on indices and cash market prices can continue without interruption. The same is true for market monitoring, which in turn supports investor protection. The market remains liquid in the sense that investors can easily turn assets, e.g., stocks, into cash and vice versa. And even if latency becomes lower and lower due to HFT and a new generation of trading systems, the safeguards and mechanisms that are needed to guarantee smooth and orderly price discovery remain the same. I think that it is fair to say that, with our safeguards in place, we at Deutsche Börse have done all that man can do to avoid an incident such as the so-called Flash Crash.

I will end with a final word about the "new landscape." While technical measures such as those just described are important safeguards against market turbulence, the central issues at stake are of a more fundamental nature. Perhaps one of the deeper reasons behind the financial crisis is the cynicism of some of those who should actually feel responsible for the pillars that make the market system work in the way that thinkers like Adam Smith, Walter Eucken or Friedrich von Hayek had believed it should work. I strongly believe in the principle of depending on healthy self-interest as opposed to lofty idealism, which all too easily becomes an excuse for authoritarianism. *However, the principle of self-interest must not be allowed to turn against the market principle itself.* That is, it must remain a principle, something that it will not do if we allow markets to become dark, opaque or exceedingly complex. This is why I believe in exchanges as regulated markets that are driven by professionalism and integrity.

Ladies and gentlemen, I thank you for your attention.

Chapter 3
May 6: Lessons Learned and Questions Raised

Moderator: Andrew Brooks, *T. Rowe Price Associates, Inc.*
Robert Gasser, *ITG*
Susan Greenglass, *Ontario Securities Commission*
Gary Katz, *International Securities Exchange*
Tim Mahoney, *BIDS Trading*
Joe Mecane, *NYSE Euronext*
William O'Brien, *Direct Edge*

ANDREW BROOKS: This has been a difficult decade for equity investors. It was a decade characterized by two generational bear markets followed by this incredible afternoon earlier this year, the Flash Crash on May 6.[1] For most of us, that afternoon highlighted what I call the dysfunction in our markets. Market innovation, regulatory frameworks, and economic incentives were not, and perhaps are still not, properly aligned to better serve investors. Investor confidence, contrary to some of the conversation that we heard earlier, has been shaken. You might not see it in the numbers. Yet people at the hardware stores, or the grocery stores, will tell you that they have been rattled by the market.

In the aftermath of May 6, there are a number of things worth reading or observing, including the CFTC-SEC[2] and Grant-Thornton reports[3] and the recent testimony and various statements of industry, academic, and other professionals in Washington and the media.

---

[1] For summary, see, Findings Regarding The Market Events of May 6, 2010, September 30, 2010. See, http://www.sec.gov/news/studies/2010/marketevents-report.pdf Also, a non-governmental account on May 6 is offered in this provocative opinion piece, one of the many commentaries on the events of May 6, Flash-Crash Story Looks More Like a Fairy Tale, Michael Bunchanan, *Bloomberg*, http://www.bloomberg.com/news/2012-05-07/flash-crash-story-looks-more-like-a-fairy-tale.html.

[2] Findings Regarding The Market Events of May 6, 2010. Report of the Staffs of the CFTC and SEC to the Joint Advisory Committee on Emerging Regulatory Issue, http://www.sec.gov/news/studies/2010/marketevents-report.pdf

[3] See, SEC-CFTC proposed trade at rule could increase expenses and reduce revenues for retail brokers, Grant Thornton, May 24, 2011 http://www.grantthornton.com/staticfiles/GTCom/Financial%20services/Financial%20Bulletin/Fin%20Bulletin_trade-at%20rule_Grant%20Thornton%20LLP.htm

Additionally, aside from the proposed rule above, there are several related regulatory rule changes, significantly the SEC FORM 13H large trader reporting which requires "self-identification," by December 1, 2011 and brokers to begin reporting any Unidentified Large Traders by April 4, 2012.

R.A. Schwartz et al. (eds.), *The Quality of Our Financial Markets: Taking Stock of Where We Stand*, Zicklin School of Business Financial Markets Series,
DOI 10.1007/978-1-4614-5592-9_3, © Springer Science+Business Media New York 2013

We have assembled a wonderful panel today to discuss the events of May 6. I have asked the speakers to check their self-interest at the door. We want them to be objective. I have asked our panel to stimulate a challenging debate that avoids unnecessary contention. In that vein, how do we adjust our market structure to promote fairness and responsible behavior and, in so doing, prevent another May 6? What lessons were learned from May 6? Robert Gasser, what did you learn from May 6?

ROBERT GASSER: Our firm has thrived on the increasing market complexity and fragmentation. Some would describe it as chaos, though I wouldn't go that far. We have thrived in that environment as an electronic provider, as a facilitator of electronic best execution for the buy-side.

We learned that there is some fragility in the US market structure. The aftermath of the Flash Crash is pretty clear. Now we are asking, is there a law of diminishing returns in the way our market has evolved? It certainly has become more efficient. Look at transaction costs analysis data. It shows a steady decline in trading costs over the past decades (with the exception of some blips for volatility).[4] There has been a steady decline in the cost of execution too, as the markets have become more electronic, and more competitive. That is all good. But the Flash Crash and recent market volatility have caused us to be a little more fragile, as I said, from a structural standpoint. We are pretty concerned.

In a recent speech to the Security Traders Association, I warned that we could have another Flash Crash.[5] We've had two over the span of 50 years.[6] That is probably acceptable to most of us. But to potentially have two over the course of a year, the first being on May 6, is pretty challenging.

You can't dispute the fact that the present 24 weeks of straight equity mutual fund outflows, according to data compiled by the Investment Company Institute –

---

[4] Behind the Drop in Trading Costs, *Traders Magazine*, January 2011, Peter Chapman http://www.tradersmagazine.com/issues/24_318/trading-costs-lyons-cronin-106923-1.html

[5] Bob Gasser, CEO of Investment Technology Group, told attendees at the Security Traders Association's 77th Annual Conference in Washington, D.C., in September 2010 that he would support fees for some message traffic. Gasser made this and other suggestions as part of his presentation describing ways he felt the industry could strive to avoid another similar May 6 Flash Crash. For one thing, Gasser suggested messaging fees could help limit traffic that doesn't add to overall market liquidity. "One thing we have been seeing is bursts of message traffic and anyone managing their own market data will tell you that the spikes are… scary during a period when there really isn't a lot of trading data," he said, referring to market data reviewed by ITG. He added that the fees could be a way to help pay for the consolidated audit trail proposed by the Securities and Exchange Commission. "Folks that participate in the behavior need to share in the burden it creates for all of us."

Gasser also mentioned rules the regulators had proposed to additionally govern dark pools, naked sponsored- access and flash orders. He also mentioned the single-stock circuit breakers, at the time in a pilot period, and agreed the SEC is right to require the exchanges to adopt the same thresholds.

Source: *Wall Street Letter*, Jeanene Timberlake, September 09, 2010:

[6] Gasser explained in a follow-up that the first "Flash Crash" occurred on May 28 1962.

See, http://www.advancedtrading.com/exchanges/225700888

after some good sequential positive inflows up to May 6 – has had a very negative effect on investor psychology. The Flash Crash created this perception that the US markets are rigged. I am not saying that they are rigged. But that is the perception. It is something that we, as an industry, including the buy-side and the sell-side – and with the regulators taking the lead – are concerned about. As an industry we need to be sure that we are acting, not only out of self-interest, but with a longer-term perspective on the health of the US capital markets and capital formation.

SUSAN GREENGLASS: My remarks are my own views and not necessarily those of the Ontario Securities Commission, or of the other Commission staff. Our SRO, the Investment Industry Regulatory Organization of Canada (IIROC), published a report last month on the events of May 6 in the Canadian marketplace.[7] We have been working closely with them on our next steps.

On May 6, the markets in Canada experienced a brief but extreme drop, similar to the US markets. The Canadian markets reacted quite rapidly to the events in the US. About two minutes after the drop in the US markets, we noticed the same in our markets. Our recovery also lagged about two minutes later than it began in the US markets. One difference between our markets that is highlighted in the IIROC report: In Canada we have an order protection obligation that extends through the full depth of the book.[8] It has been historically a feature in equity markets in Canada. We have had multiple marketplaces since 2005.[9] As a result of the full depth of book protection, as the IROC report notes, the price dislocation that we observed was not as significant in Canada as it was in the US because all available liquidity had to be taken out at all price levels.[10]

GARY KATZ: There are three lessons that I hope we can take away from May 6. One is that liquidity is not guaranteed. However, it is something that investors over time have come to expect and believe will always be there. But liquidity is a fragile animal. Another lesson from May 6 is this: What we have come to expect will always be there, can very quickly disappear. In other words, there is an expectation

---

[7]Review of the Market Events of May 6, 2010, IIROC, http://sdocs.iiroc.ca/English/Documents/2010/C6CB526F-9325-4DED-9F4F-98CDCB935FF3_en.pdf.

[8]As the Canadian Securities Administrators noted in October 2008, in their rulemaking on trade-through protection: "This approach is different from the one adopted in Regulation NMS in the United States, which provides protection only to the best bid and offer on each marketplace (top-of-book)."

[9]The rules finalized by lawmakers in Canada in 2001 to provide the framework for multiple marketplaces, took effect in 2005.

[10]"It is also important to note the trade through obligation in Canada is a "full depth of book" obligation. As such, orders in Canada could not bypass any visible, better-priced orders on other marketplaces and the price decreases were slowed until all liquidity was exhausted. This should be contrasted with the situation in the US where order migration from some of the markets that employed volatility controls or experienced market data issues was significant and the securities traded to increasingly lower levels without the obligation to trade with all better-priced orders in transparent markets."

Source: Page 17, Review of the Market Events of May 6, 2010, IIROC, http://sdocs.iiroc.ca/English/Documents/2010/C6CB526F-9325-4DED-9F4F-98CDCB935FF3_en.pdf

that if you want to sell a security someone will be there standing ready to buy. That is not what happened on May 6. What we saw were a lot of trades taking place, far from the market even at prices like one cent because the typical layers of the order book had been pulled out of the market. The third lesson is the importance of coordination among exchanges. That is something the options exchanges do extremely well. Fragmentation is not necessarily bad. We have eight options[11] exchanges competing with each other. They are trying to pull market share away from each other and beat each other's brains out while at the same time recognizing that coordination among all the exchanges is critical to ensuring that investors have confidence in the markets.

Finally, I would like to compliment Steve Wunsch[12], who is sitting in front of me. His papers have recognized something that is critically important. Namely, that decisions made by regulators are very important in market structure. They can impact our businesses, not one year later, but many, many years later. The enactment of some decisions may be long forgotten. Yet now we are seeing the impact today of those same decisions that were made ten years ago, or fifteen years ago.

We can't look at high-frequency trading (HFT) and say that HFT started three years ago and caused what is now happening to our markets. We need to look back further to far-reaching regulatory decisions that led to Reg NMS, penny trading, and the order handling rules, and that ultimately changed our market structure. We seem to have forgotten about them.

JOE MECANE: I learned from May 6 how many shuttle flights there are per day between here and Washington talking to regulators! (laughter). Seriously, I would highlight three things that May 6 underlined. One echoes Gary's point, the interconnectedness of the markets and products. We all know that is part of many arbitrage strategies, that is trading across different products to find mis-pricings. My first point is about providing liquidity across different products such as equities and options and futures, in other words, liquidity strategies that are linked across all the different exchanges. As noted already, what we take for granted as being there – liquidity – is not always guaranteed most of the day. It is important to look at that, not only in the context of individual markets and individual products, but also across those different products. That then becomes something that we need to incorporate in any rules or rulemaking on trading in individual products. That means, in effect, that the rules for one product may need to factor in the fact that there may be strategies linked to other markets.

Secondly, May 6 also highlighted the need for markets and participants to take a pause at certain points in time to let liquidity re-aggregate, to let judgment enter into the equation. We have always had pauses on the New York Stock Exchange. The obvious fact about May 6 is that there wasn't any market-wide mechanism for

[11] For update as of May 2012, see Exchange Fatigue, *Traders Magazine*, May 2012, Peter Chapman http://www.tradersmagazine.com/issues/25_337/nasdaq-options-exchange-109992-1.html

[12] Wunch, the self-proclaimed and well-respected libertarian thinker, and an advocate of limited government, is the principal inventor of the electronic Arizona Stock Exchange, now defunct, and of the ISE Stock Exchange.

judgment to enter into the equation. That is, there was no pause that would allow a trader's judgment to be introduced into trading and the price determination process. So, the circuit breakers were the first step towards a market-wide mechanism to accomplish a re-aggregation.[13]

In a world where we are measuring individual transactions in a millionth of a second, clearly there will be times when liquidity won't aggregate fast enough, when the matching engines will be operating faster than the liquidity can replenish itself and come back. Therefore, one of the safeguards that is unavoidable in a microsecond-type world is a pause mechanism.

My final point is the need for a better harmonized regulatory structure· The fact that it took five months to compile the May 6 report[14], was reflective of two things: the complexity at stake, and the desire of the SEC to get to the bottom of what happened and then reconstruct one 20-minute period of May 6, in a pretty complex environment.

The time period of this reconstruction was also exasperated by the fact that aggregated data didn't exist and had to be created. Those of you who were at the SIFMA[15] market structure committee conference last week heard some of the SEC statement about how long and how onerous it was to re-aggregate that data. Because the aggregated market data didn't exist and needed to be constructed. Indeed, our regulatory structure, which is moving toward a more unified, harmonized structure, isn't there yet. For example, there is still no consolidated audit trail which was actually proposed before May 6[16] – this all underscores the fact that moving in this unified direction is important from a structural standpoint.[17]

WILLIAM O'BRIEN: I learned two lessons from May 6. Part of that first lesson stems from a trend over the past decade. And we really don't spend a lot of time talking about it. The exchanges have the ability to add value to the trading process, to enhance, and to improve the business models of their customers who are brokers in most cases – In the end, the exchange can add this value and improve the process for investors who are also their customers. The exchanges have recognized, sometimes more than others, that they historically have performed a lot of utility functions. When should the stock market be open and when it should be closed? When

[13]For a summary of SEC regulatory action in this matter, see, Two Years After Flash Crash, SEC Still Pursuing New Safeguards, *Institutional Investor*, May 11, 2012, Michael Peltz, http://www.institutionalinvestor.com/Article/3023836/Two-Years-After-Flash-Crash-SEC-Still-Pursuing-New-Safeguards.html

[14]Findings Regarding The Market Events of May 6, 2010. Report of the states of the CFTC and SEC to the joint advisory committee on emerging regulatory issue, http://www.sec.gov/news/studies/2010/marketevents-report.pdf

[15]Securities Industry and Financial Markets Association.

[16]Consolidated Audit Trail Rule Imminent, *Traders Magazine*, John D'Antona Jr. http://www.tradersmagazine.com/news/sec-consolidated-audit-trail-q1-109796-1.html

[17]In the context of Mecane's remarks, recommended reading is the testimony of Larry Leibowitz, chief operating officer of NYSE Euronext before the House Financial Services Subcommittee on Capital Markets, Insurance and Government Sponsored Enterprises, May 11, 2010. http://www.house.gov/apps/list/hearing/financialsvcs_dem/leibowitz_5.11.10.pdf

things are so out of control that, from a liquidity aggregation and price discovery perspective, it should be closed? That is one of the utility functions we have often looked at exchanges to provide and address. What hit everybody over the head on May 6 was that we had not spent enough time in applying adequate technology to that responsibility. Of course, technology has been of enormous benefit to investors. How do we evolve that utility function to account for those times when the markets should cease to be open because they are no longer fair and orderly?

How do we apply that to the more egalitarian competitive market structure that has served our nation so well? This is a market structure that takes the hyperbolic increase in the rate of trading from a speed perspective into account. You talk about the pause on the New York Stock Exchange. The New York Stock Exchange didn't universally apply it. The NYSE was running three markets on May 6: the NYSE itself, NYSE Arca and NYSE Amex. One of them, the NYSE had a pause; but it didn't pause its other two markets. Now amplify that across the entire market, not only to encompass all exchanges, but also to encompass the variety of other value-added execution services – such as the availability of brokers and dark pools off the exchange. That amplification produces real inconsistency about how to handle a crisis situation. This failure – the lack of marketwide coordination in terms of circuit breakers on May 6 was unfortunate, in many ways. It was embarrassingly exposed on May 6.

The second lesson that I learned on May 6 is that you can actually address those aforementioned issues fairly quickly and without a lot of deconstruction in the parts of our market that work very well. I take a different view of what Bob Gasser said earlier. I think the risk of another May 6 has gone down substantially given the market structure reforms that we have already implemented since then. We have done this in a very, very short period of time. The notion of thousands of stocks going from $40.00 one minute to a penny the next, to $39 the next, cannot really happen now given how the single stock circuit breakers are working, at least in the S&P stocks and some active ETFs. These are the names that are covered in the single stock circuit breaker reforms enacted since the Flash Crash.[18]

We certainly have a ways to go on that and on other aspects of market infrastructure. Still, there is a fairly high degree of consensus, at least among the exchanges, about the infrastructure improvements we need. And there is not a lot of talk about how we would start to implement reforms that would restrict, impede, slow, or otherwise harm the ability of people to innovate, whether it is in a proprietary trading model or in an agency trading model.

BROOKS: Direct Edge is now an exchange. Can you halt trading in a stock? Can you call somebody and say, I need to stop trading in a stock, right now?

O'BRIEN: Yes, we have the ability to cease trading in a stock.

BROOKS: Does it apply to the other markets as well, or only to yours?

---

[18]For a summary of SEC regulatory action in this matter, see, Two Years After Flash Crash, SEC Still Pursuing New Safeguards, *Institutional Investor*, May 11, 2012, Michael Peltz, http://www.institutionalinvestor.com/Article/3023836/Two-Years-After-Flash-Crash-SEC-Still-Pursuing-New-Safeguards.html

O'BRIEN: No. First of all, you have to look at the rationale and at your obligations. The NYSE and NASDAQ are the markets where companies historically had publicly listed themselves. These are our listing markets historically. I won't say they are our "primary" listing markets anymore, because there isn't a primary market any more. In any event, part of the service you provide to investors on behalf of the issuers is a notification of a listing, and of a single stock halt when there is a company specific event, or relevant news from some other event. That service works.

The issuers often pay exchanges hundreds of thousands of dollars in listing fees. I don't think anyone finds any problem with that today. Then there is the question of how to address a trading imbalance, whether that is caused by fundamental or non-fundamental reasons. On May 6 we might have had a combination of both. In many respects, it was a good, old-fashioned panic. What is the right way for price re-aggregation and price discovery, or a validation that a price discovery event needs to occur? Sometimes, as we have seen since May 6 many of the events, simply put, are the result of clearly erroneous trades. That is just another aspect of market structure, of infrastructure that needs improvement. There is no single exchange-based or single market center-based halt mechanism that could work to address those issues. On May 6, it was, in effect every exchange, every broker, every investor for themselves, because there was no market-wide mechanism to help curb the Flash Crash. That approach clearly doesn't work. We have gone a long way to addressing that since then. Of course, it has to be done collectively by the industry.

BROOKS: We have dozens of market centers and execution venues. In this environment, do market makers have an obligation on where stocks are trading?

O'BRIEN: This is an infrastructure issue. Let's be honest. When we had monopoly exchanges[19] that were performing this utility function to some degree, the mechanism for controlling price discovery didn't always work. I can't over-state that. There were stock market panics in 1907, in 1929, in 1962 in 1987. I don't think anyone came away from them saying that the mechanism for controlling prices in these panics worked particularly well at these monopoly exchanges. No amount of privilege will adequately compensate a market participant – that is, a specialist or market maker – to absorb the kind of risk we had in these historic panics even though these participants aim for a profit. You can't simply say that these panics won't occur again if you compensate a market maker and specialist to absorb the risk. The market at large needs to settle on the appropriate procedures for validating price discovery

BROOKS: Gary, you had the opportunity to build from scratch an options exchange that was electronic, and it was connected. What questions were raised from your market that might apply to the equity markets in our May 6 experience?

KATZ: It was a unique experience to take a previously floor-based mechanism of trading and convert it into a fully-electronic marketplace.[20] Some of the

---

[19] On a national level in the US, the "monopoly" exchanges and markets he refers to were the New York Stock Exchange, American Stock Exchange and later NASDAQ.

[20] See History of ISE, http://www.ise.com/WebForm/viewPage.aspx?categoryId=504

requirements that we are talking about and suggesting today – for example, a market maker obligation – were carried through from the floor-based markets to our all-electronic market. We at the ISE are a good example of whether that actually works. All of the market makers at ISE are required to provide continuous, two-sided markets at all times. On May 6 they didn't, and at other times they don't.[21] They are the equivalent of the high-frequency trader that we talked about so much today. They have very sensitive systems designed to smell when there is a problem, when information is not flowing properly, and when there is a disconnect between market places. The market makers initially widen their markets, and then they remove their quotes from the markets. Yet, they have an obligation to make a two-sided market.

Let me ask you a question: What is the size of the fine I would have to put in place to require them to stay there and go out of business? If you remove your quotes from the market, you now have to give me your entire business. Because ultimately that is the decision you are asking them to make – stay there and go out of business. They will make the same decision each and every time. In an earlier panel, somebody compared this to standing in the way of a freight train. You hear the other analogy of catching a falling knife. Market makers are not there to provide liquidity continuously in all market circumstances. A mechanism needs to be put in place that allows the market maker to gracefully stop making markets in line and with all the markets together.

One of the aspects of the options market as a derivatives market is that when the underlying market halts a particular stock, all the options exchanges halt trading in that option. There is no debate. We don't compete with each other in that area. We all stop trading instantaneously. A message is sent out by the primary market, or listings market (or whatever you want to call it), and when that message is sent out electronically, all the options exchanges halt trading.

This goes back to my earlier point. We are coordinated and, for that very brief moment in time, we stop competing with each other because the bigger picture is more important. In other words, we want the investor to come back in five minutes, the next day, or the next year. Whatever money one exchange might make while all the others close is insignificant relative to the investor confidence that would be lost.

BROOKS: The real challenge is to retain the confidence of investors, to get them back into the market quickly. If you are counting on somebody else's capital to provide a market and to make a market, you are playing a loser's game.

GREENGLASS: In our jurisdiction, we have one market regulator who is responsible for monitoring trading across all markets – and that is the IIROC, which is an SRO, or Self-Regulatory Organization The IIROC has the ability and the authority to halt a security across all markets. But there are no single stock circuit breakers in

[21]Market makers do have this obligation at the ISE. In fact, they are fined and sanctioned if they pull their quote in certain instances. Katz is saying that market makers would rather pay these fines in periods of market stress and volatility rather than lose potentially more in capital and money by continually posting their two-sides quotes.

place in Canada that can be implemented on a rapid basis across all markets. That is something we are taking a look at.[22] Additionally, we are also looking at some of the controls that exist for erroneous orders. What was highlighted does not work as effectively as it should because those are not coordinated among markets.

BROOKS: It is impressive that we came up with the circuit breaker response in the US in a pretty timely manner. The moral hazard issue in the market place is interesting. Maybe that leads us to questions raised regarding order routing practices. Bob, what about economic incentives for market participants, such as payment for order flow, rebating, and internalization practices? Are there challenges with that model?

On May 6, somebody routed away from a lot of markets to get Accenture temporarily down to a penny a share from $41.00 a share. By the way, if you go into Bloomberg you can't get that price anymore. It has been expunged. It went down to a penny. If you were an Accenture shareholder, it looked like your stock went to one cent! Bob?

GASSER: There was a lot of data expunged.[23] The SEC had a hard time reconstructing the day, as you pointed out earlier. There are a couple of things that can be said. For one thing, there are homogenized liquidity strategies amongst broker/dealers, certainly among smart routers. There is an arms race in smart routers. It is probably a little bit more centered on latency. Everyone in this business is confronted with the same challenge. You want to have something that is robust in terms of its ability to store and track data. You want something that facilitates low-latency access. Because the market has become a place in which chasing those aberrational quotes or flickering quotes is a big challenge.[24]

There was an element of that quote chasing on May 6. Smart routing is the base line infrastructure that you need to compete in the algorithmic trading business.[25] The algorithms themselves have some homogenization as well. But, those smart routing techniques and strategies and production environments operated with eerie similarity on May 6.[26] It is interesting; it is almost a generational thing. This

[22] See, Guidance Respecting the Implementation of Single-Stock Circuit Breakers, IIROC, Feb. 2, 2012, http://sdocs.iiroc.ca/English/Documents/2012/7cf90cce-57ae-4760-822a-46b1525e2051_en.pdf

[23] Since there was no industry-wide consolidated audit trail on May 6 that necessitated much more expansive data storage, some market data from May 6 was not retained. It was "expunged." Generally, however, financial services firms keep market information as required by regulators.

[24] High frequency trading strategies often involve "pinging" – sending out hundreds of IOC (immediate or cancel) orders or bid/ask quotes which are good for only milliseconds. They are trying to sniff out a "real" order, i.e. a big slow-moving order by a non-HFT trader. These are the aberrational or flickering quotes Gasser is referring to. Some analysts say they create an illusion of deep liquidity when in fact it's mainly "noise."

[25] See, Smart Order Routing Systems Getting Smarter, John Dodge, *Securities Technology Monitor*, April 5, 2010, http://www.securitiestechnologymonitor.com/issues/22_7/-25026-1.html

[26] Many algorithms and smart routers are "commoditized," Gasser explains. Thus, each VWAP algo from several brokers operates much the same. Gassers point is that these "plain vanilla" algos and smart routers tended to operate in lockstep during the Flash Crash.

arms race has spawned a community of folks who have grown up in this business. They are relatively young and they haven't seen things like May 6 before. They haven't seen volatility like that before. They treated the delayed response of market data from an exchange as a technical aberration and then moved on to the next one, and then onto the next one, until they probably hit a stub quote or an erroneous trade or two.[27] That homogenization, to Bill's point earlier, is one of the things that we are concerned about.

We are moving toward congruity in terms of circuit breakers amongst listed exchanges. But there is still a herd mentality that is very dependent on market data, which is now exploding everywhere. Market data, despite today's low volume, is exploding in terms of the infrastructure needed to process it. If you have gaps in market data, you trigger aberrational trading decisions in reaction to that. Now that we have this homogenized, smart routed, algorithmically traded world, there is the potential for folks to move in a herd toward the price point that may be inaccurate. And that leads to another price point that is inaccurate which leads to more price points that are inaccurate, and so on. And before you know it, you are blowing through even a tightened stub quote. In other words, if you trade off of bad market data, then your trade gets reported to the tape, then another algo trades off that new reference price your trade created, and so on. It is like the dominoes falling.

That was the nature of my concern. But, that model, that maker-taker economic model was all incentivized to reduce brokers' expenses. A lot of that reduction has been passed on to the investors.[28] Institutions are as cut- throat as ever in terms of pricing. It is not as if we are sitting here basking in the glow of improved operating margins. We are just keeping pace.

BROOKS: We ought to be mindful of how we define a market maker, and what that definition means in an electronic world that moves in nano-seconds. Is a market maker somebody who puts out a quote that is accessible? If you are in the game and you are putting out quotes, bids and offers, and they are not accessible because you cancel them so quickly, I am not sure that ties in with the definition.

ROB RICHARDSON (Zicklin School of Business) From the Floor: Has the added use and creation of – leveraged ETFs – index-sector based ETFs, and options based on those ETFs – created a more volatile and risk – induced scenario in a market making event, based on news that makes the trading on those underlyings across a fragmented market a lot more difficult to handle?

BROOKS: The SEC may have weighed in on some of these leveraged ETFs in terms of their appropriateness for investors. They are pretty scary instruments. They are pretty scary in terms of their derivative impact on the market.

KATZ: I would like to go back to one of the fundamental differences between options market structure and equities market structure. It talks to what Joe just raised. It is what you are hearing a lot more about today from leaders of regulated

[27] Stub quotes are bids for stocks near zero. For example, $0.01 bid for a stock trading at $25.00. Erroneous trades are errors due to mistakes on the part of one of the counterparties, incorrect or stale market data.

[28] This is referring to the rebate strategies operated by market centers such as ECNs and ATS.

exchanges. That is, the removal from the marketplace of order flow into the dark pools. That removal of order flow doesn't occur in the options market. From the start of options trading in the US, all options are cleared through the Options Clearing Corporation. All listed options must be traded on an exchange. There is no dark pool, so the good flow has not been removed from the marketplace. As a result, we don't have to make our market provide liquidity. They are motivated to provide liquidity because they get to interact with all of the flow. Some flow has less knowledge in it, so our liquidity providers are able to make markets for that flow. And mixing information-based flow together with the more 'informationless' flow will support a more profitable business. That is why they are there. We can't require people to provide liquidity if they don't make money.

When you move over to the equity world, you hear statements like, "12 percent to 30 percent is in the dark pools," and terms like "fragmented." Let me ask a question. What percentage of the good flow has been removed from the market? It is not 12 percent to 30 percent. It is, 100 percent! That is why it is there. When you remove that from a distribution, what you are left with is flow that is very difficult to trade with.

You've heard the term exhaust.[29] That is what you are asking liquidity providers to trade with on a regular basis. That is why we don't see the same liquidity providers in the equities market that we saw years ago. The good flow has been removed. If you want market makers or specialists to make two-sided continuous markets, whether they are there standing in the crowd, or doing it electronically, you have to allow them to trade with all of the flow for the best results.

Of course, there is a place for large block size trades, and that can be done in a dark environment.

You certainly don't want to take all of the flow and force it back to an exchange. Because that again recreates a problem of market impact. In any event, the retail flow that is so important for liquidity providers to trade with right now is absent from the regulated exchanges.

O'BRIEN: When I think of off exchange flow, I put it in three buckets: The first is the classic internalization bucket. You could have a legitimate debate about that practice. You can make an argument that it is a different product, that this segment of the market's order flow can say it is less informed than other segments of order flow. However, I can get some benefits out of that by routing to an internalizer with guaranteed 2000-share market order executions; guaranteed price improvement and other benefits. Of course, in that sense it is a different product.

The second bucket is the automation of more traditional institutional agency models. ITG started this trend many years ago. Then, thirdly, other firms that once had a floor presence with a bunch of sales traders replaced them with a computer server and a cool marketing brochure. A lot of those same floor operations have

[29] Some traders regard the order flow that is handled directly by a stock exchange as "exhaust," it is regarded as inferior to the order flow traded off the exchange.

now been completely automated. To this end, you see an alternative network evolving in the growth of electronic execution providers and ECNs.

I don't have a problem with all of this. I don't think any market should really be required to become an exchange. However, if you start to evolve a business model that takes on an exchange-like function – especially as it has become easier and faster to do – then maybe you shouldn't qualify for the lower level of regulation that they currently enjoy as a non-exchange.

MECANE: The retail question is just a cost benefit. Clearly there is a benefit to the retail firms and to the internalizers who are able to interact with those different flows. At the same time, there is a cost to the overall marketplace in terms of creating those two distinct venues for trading equities. Certainly the biggest impact to the exchange is the toxicity that Gary noted and Bill referenced. That is a legitimate issue the industry needs to debate. On the ATS automation of brokers issues, we have been black and white in terms of whether venues that are performing the same exact function should be subject to different rules and oversight. Our view is clearly with Reg ATS which was intended to create a very low barrier of entry for new entrants to come into the marketplace to break down the duopoly structure that existed until recent years.[30] Now that we have 40 different places trading equities, do you really need to create that low barrier of entry for more new entrants to come in and do exactly what an exchange does but under a different regulatory framework? We would argue that if people are performing the identical function, they should be subject to the same level of oversight.

DAVID WOODWARD (Pipeline Trading Systems): I enjoy hearing how the option exchanges all work together. The cash equity exchanges work together but, in my 25 years in the business, every crash I have seen has been led by the futures. This one, it seems, is the result of the same thing. I see Bill is smiling. Where is the cooperation between CFTC and the SEC in terms of making sure a futures-led crash doesn't happen again?

GREENGLASS: In the IROC report, they did not see a link between the futures and options markets and the decline in the equity markets.[31] Our experience is different than that. It was really a reaction to volatility.

BROOKS: There isn't any doubt that our market needs to be more closely aligned and regulated across all asset classes. It took four months for the SEC and CFTC to deliver this report. But questions still remain: Do we need some kind of a consolidated audit trail? Do we need to understand exactly who everybody is who is coming to the teller's window asking for money?

PROFESSOR JIM ANGEL (Georgetown University) From the Floor: What I take away from May 6 is that our market is a complex network. When it is stressed with an overwhelming barrage of activity, this complex network fails in strange and weird ways. We saw this not only on May 6 but as far back as 33 years ago when the

---

[30] New York Stock Exchange and NASDAQ.

[31] Review of the Market Events of May 6, 2010, IIROC, http://sdocs.iiroc.ca/English/Documents/2010/C6CB526F-9325-4DED-9F4F-98CDCB935FF3_en.pdf

printers were jamming on the New York Stock Exchange, which led to confusion. We saw it happen in 1912, 1929 and then in 1961. If I look at market history, the lesson that I take away is that our market has a finite capacity. When this capacity is exceeded the market fails in ugly ways. So what we need are mechanisms to deal with this inevitable reality. When you have a dam you have spillways to deal with excess water flow. Indeed, we put in these circuit breakers. By the way, I had recommended them in April before the Flash Crash.

I would like to hear the panel's thoughts on whether a limit up, limit down mechanism would work better in our markets.

MECANE: I think that is something the exchanges and the SEC are exploring. It certainly is a more elegant methodology from this standpoint: It doesn't stop trading the way the circuit breaker does. As we are developing the methodology, we need to be very cognizant of the potential negatives to the limit up, limit down approach.[32] First, you run the risk of creating confusion when you are in a limit up, limit down position. That is, the market will not necessarily know what it going on. Second, is the issue of whether you interfere with price discovery because you have quotes in the marketplace when a stock is looking to re-price? The fact is that this might not necessary be the right price at which to trade. I think they are surmountable problems, but, nevertheless, we need to keep them in mind as we formulate a solution.

O'BRIEN: Jim Angel's analogy about the dam is good. We have all grappled with this as we have managed our systems. If you are going to have a failure, have a hard failure. The worst kind of failure is a soft failure, where it is part operational, or part not. With a soft failure, you can have some really bad consequences, and it is analogous to May 6.

With regard to limit up limit down, I will echo some of Joe's points in a different way. It is all about the problem you are trying to solve. We have some experience now to (hopefully) get us to a better solution. We clearly need a better system-wide reboot mechanism. The circuit breaker pretty much does that. You can say that it should be 12 percent not 8 percent, and that we should be closed for this period of time rather than that period of time. The question that we've faced since then is, when does that reboot button get pushed? Is it getting pushed now in ways that really doesn't make a lot of sense? What should be done when one irrational, or otherwise erroneous trade, is made over the counter? What should be done when some exchange executions occur that satisfies its minimum obligation to route to other exchanges, but then rips so far through its own book that the circuit breaker gets triggered?

Any limit up, limit down mechanism that I have heard of ultimately results in a circuit breaker. It is not a replacement of one with the other. There are times when you are really having a meltdown and will need a market-wide price discovery event

---

[32] Mecane is referring to price limits on some stocks that would temporarily stop trading if they traded outside pre-defined limits. For a summary of SEC regulatory action in this matter, see, Two Years After Flash Crash, SEC Still Pursuing New Safeguards, Michael Peltz, *Institutional Investor* http://www.institutionalinvestor.com/Article/3023836/Two-Years-After-Flash-Crash-SEC-Still-Pursuing-New-Safeguards.html

that only a pause can provide. Of course, you can layer on top, or inside that circuit breaker some limit up, limit down type mechanism so that the circuit breaker is not tripped unnecessarily.

DAVID WEILD (Capital Markets Advisory Partners) From the Floor: I want to follow up on something that Joe alluded to about small and micro-cap stocks, and how they are trading differently. At these conferences, I notice an almost unilateral focus on large-cap S&P 500. As far as I know, there is only one volatility index: the VIX.[33] There is a very different experience for small- and micro-cap stocks compared to large cap-stocks. The following question was posed to the exchange officials at the recent regulatory panel hearings in Washington on the events of May 6: How is market structure affecting liquidly in small- and micro-cap stocks? People suddenly had to stop and ponder this question. The answer was very clear: Small- and micro-cap stocks have actually lost liquidity in the aggregate, and most would agree that large-caps stocks have gained liquidity. It is interesting to note that the median market value of listed company in this country is only 350 million dollars, which is reflective of the micro-cap sector. In light of this I would like to ask, what are we doing, or what can we do, to improve the liquidity creation mechanisms around small and micro-cap stocks?

I hear anecdotally that there is no longer any institutional liquidity in small-cap stocks. What can we do to put some focus on this problem to get the market to breathe life back into that area that is critical to capital formation, job growth, and US competitiveness?

O'BRIEN: Great question, we are actually talking about how to improve the American economy. I love questions like that because they are all too infrequent. I go back to my original remark about how I viewed Direct Edge as American's newest stock exchange. We are a firm that can really innovate and enhance the experience for the trading customers, and potentially for issuers. There are some limitations on that right now.

Reg NMS can serve at times to effectively restrict exchanges given that Reg NMS treats the micro-cap stock the same way that it treats large-caps like Citigroup in terms of how it should trade and the increments in which it should trade. I don't know if that monolithic approach makes sense. We can't breach the confidence of the nation's investors, and we have to be very careful how we modify our market structure. But there are improvements to both the trading and the listing regulatory infrastructure that can provide for more flexibility to improve the quality of the capital markets for smaller companies.

BROOKS: I want to follow up on the sense that the investing public might have about getting equal access and fairness. That might be particularly evident in the small-cap arena. It might be worthwhile to figure out if we should have some separate sandboxes for small-caps.

In small-caps, you need friction. You need to pay people to talk about stocks, to promote them in a positive way, to tell the story. They don't happen on their own.

---

[33] The Chicago Board Options Exchange Market Volatility Index.

The CNBC crowd doesn't get to the 125 million dollar micro-cap stock that might be the next Hewlett Packard or something. That is worth examining. As a big, small, and mid-cap investor at T Rowe Price, if we got better markets, better liquidity, better service, better access, better true volume, if we got all of this together, then we might be willing to pay a little more to trade small caps. Not that we are out there all the time and want to pay more.

Is that something that investors, at any level, institutional or retail, should be willing to do?

GASSER: One of the most interesting parts of the CFTC and SEC report on the Flash Crash[34] is the section on electronic market makers. Here you have a free market mechanism in terms of electronic market making. These guys are paying retail houses to take in their order flow. They are paid to take risk. It is a very pure free-market mechanism. Obviously their decision is based on the environment that we've gone over ad nauseam. They decided that they would not take that risk anymore, and that they were going to route these orders as market orders. I think there was quite a bit of market order flow. That is a very legitimate question to be asking at this stage of the game. In some institutions, I don't think they have ever seen a market held order. It is always a market not held order. But, clearly, in the retail space, there are significant vestiges of that left, as evidenced by the data that the SEC poured through. I was actually surprised by some of that.

MECANE: I don't know if that solves the actual fundamental issue. Whether you have a market order or an aggressive limit order, you can end up with the same sort of damage. It highlights more of an order handling issue as well as the fragmentation issue that we talked about earlier insofar as liquidity is not aggregated together. Someone routed an order to the market to sell stock at a penny, or to buy stock at 10,000 dollar or whatever it was.

We have all been spoiled because the markets are generally liquid. You can send an order into the marketplace and, 99.9 percent of the time, you will get a decent execution. Fragmentation issues and the different pools of liquidity aside, what May 6 shows is this: You have to have another level of diligence at play when you look at liquidity in the marketplace before you send an order into the market and assume you will get a decent execution back.

BROOKS: There is this concept of fire and forget! You put an order in an algorithmic model and you fire it off and forget about it. That is a pretty dangerous thing to do today. As we conclude, I would ask you all to think about this. How would you feel if we lost a generation of investors? Can we challenge order routing practices? What happens when no one owns the quote? Was the stock market a fairer and better

---

[34] For summary, see, Findings Regarding The Market Events of May 6, 2010, September 30, 2010. See, http://www.sec.gov/news/studies/2010/marketevents-report.pdf. Also, a non-governmental account on May 6 is offered in this provocative opinion piece, one of the many commentaries on the events of May 6, Flash-Crash Story Looks More Like a Fairy Tale, Michael Bunchanan, *Bloomberg News*, http://www.bloomberg.com/news/2012-05-07/flash-crash-story-looks-more-like-a-fairy-tale.html

place 20 years ago? How would you rate the industry's response to May 6? Is technology the problem? When is fast too fast? Do we need a consolidated audit trail? Should all orders be tagged? What do we do about cancellation rates that are greater than 90 percent? What does it mean if your model is dependent on volume growth?

Thank you, all. This was a great panel. (Applause)

Chapter 4
The Needs of the Buy-Side: How Well Are They Being Met?

Moderator: Rob Shapiro, *Bloomberg Tradebook LLC*
Alfred Eskandar, *Liquidnet*
Marie Konstance, *Nomura Securities International, Inc.*
Matt Lyons, *Capital Research and Management Company*
Mary McDermott-Holland, *NASDAQ OMX*
David Palmer, *Hudson Bay Capital Management*
Alan Hill, *Jones Trading Institutional Services*

ROB SHAPIRO: You might find it odd that we have a panel entitled, "*The Needs of the Buy-side: How Well Are They Being Met?*" Why? Because we have only one buy-side person on the panel! We did the pre-conference call and wondered aloud, Oh, poor Matt Lyons, the little lamb on the buy-side, will be surrounded by all these lions! I reminded them, however, that this is an 800-pound lamb. So, I am not quite sure he is at risk.

For the record, I spent half of my career on the buy-side. Marie Konstance spent the better part, if not all of her career, on the buy-side. So, some of the panelists, and your faithful moderator, do have some buy-side Street credentials.

We will start off with liquidity. Are the liquidity needs of the buy-side being met today? Just use your buzzers. (laughter) Kidding.

MATT LYONS: I have been on the buy-side for 15 years. Generally, I think that the liquidity needs of an institutional investor are being fundamentally met. The panelists earlier talked about markets breaking down during the liquidity crisis of 2007 to 2008, and the subsequent freezing of some fixed-income markets. Yet the equity markets remained open and accessible during this period. That was something a lot of people lost focus on. It points to what is going right in the market. Volume has increased. Spreads have come down. The sell-side community has worked very hard to meet the liquidity needs of the buy-side. It is difficult at times; but overall, liquidity is available. Sometimes it is available at a price, but you usually can get in and out of positions. That is fundamentally a good thing.

SHAPIRO: Has the context of liquidity changed much since the Flash Crash of May 6[1]? In plain English, are you using more or less capital? Are you trading more or less blocks? How has liquidity sourcing changed?

---

[1] The May 6, 2010 Flash Crash saw the Dow Jones Industrial Average plunged about 1,000 points—or about 9 %—only to recover its losses within minutes. It was the second largest point swing, 1,010.14 points, and the largest 1 day point decline, 998.5 points, on an intraday basis in Dow history.

R.A. Schwartz et al. (eds.), *The Quality of Our Financial Markets: Taking Stock of Where We Stand*, Zicklin School of Business Financial Markets Series, DOI 10.1007/978-1-4614-5592-9_4,

LYONS: Our observation is that the cost of capital has been extremely expensive[2] since after the crisis. We were probably being offered it more than most from the stories I've heard. Brokers were still willing to offer us the use of capital as principal to facilitate transactions. We were not frozen out of access to capital, which is what was happening in the fixed-income market in some products. It was a little too costly for us so we didn't take advantage of it as much as most. The way in which we have sourced liquidity has changed dramatically over the course of the last five years. Overall, block trading with the traditional broker as the intermediary negotiating the trade has decreased, certainly from most of our counterparts. Conversely, block trading through buy-side to buy-side electronic crossing networks has increased dramatically year over year.

SHAPIRO: Was the cost expressed as the spread away from the NBBO[3]?

LYONS: Yes, that is exactly it.

SHAPIRO: A lot of people are mystified or curious about what has been happening to electronic block trading. I am not sure that the statistics I have seen support the view that it has gone up. Most data suggests that overall it is on the wane. Is this is a cyclical or secular trend?

ESKANDAR: Actually, overall volumes in the market continue to baffle us. Think about it. You saw 8 billion shares going across the tape yesterday, and 10½ billion on Friday, so that 10½ billion feels like a normal day, reminding us of the higher average daily volumes – around 9½ billion to 10½ billion shares – prior to the present downturn in volume A typical day now sees volume of between 6½ billion to 7 billion shares. But, according to slides presented at the conference this morning, we are now in the normal volume range.

However, you have a lot of participants, namely high-frequency traders, coming in and out of the market, who could put up 200 to 300 million shares themselves and walk away. They are flat at the end of the trading day, at the close of the market. The Street is then left thinking that this volume today is somehow normal! But think about investors' sentiments in the market vs. the activity in the market. The two are dislocated. I don't believe that you can look at absolute figures on block trading venues, electronic or otherwise, and then take a portion of that overall volume and say, "Okay, that portion is really going up, or going down." Because, on any given day, high-frequency accounts or other types of strategies that are very active, will push up or down the overall volumes. But, as I said, this is dislocated from investors' sentiments.

It is really important to dissect volumes. Is this overall market activity? Is this investor driven? What is driving the viewpoint of a stock in the Street? Is it high-frequency traders? We lose track of that all the time. We see lots of stories on CNBC

---

[2] The cost of capital is reflected in the bid ask spread for principal transactions when brokers are using their balance sheet to facilitate block transactions.

[3] NBBO: National Best Bid and Offer, a term applying to the SEC requirement that brokers must guarantee customers the best available ask price when they buy securities and the best available bid price when they sell securities. Source: Investopedia.

and elsewhere talking about volume explosion, market droughts, etc.. If this panel is really about the needs of the buy-side, let's articulate what those needs are first. Then let's dissect them, one by one. Because I think it gets lost.

To me, an institutional investor has been the cousin you don't want to talk about in the sense that you forget about him. You focus on the topic of the day, what is really hot; you forget about the needs of the market, the overall purpose. What is the whole nature of the stock exchange? What is it supposed to deliver? What are the responsibilities of each of the venues? What are the definitions of each of the participants? Then we just group everything up. Let's talk about specific things with a specific purpose.

MARIE KONSTANCE: Al, don't you think some of this has to do with volatility? It seems like this is the kind of market where traders have been afraid to pick their spots for fear of picking a particularly bad moment to trade. Block trading isn't going to completely disappear – ever.

ESKANDAR: Absolutely. We've seen that too. In periods of high volatility, we've seen the blocks become smaller. We've seen a very direct correlation between the VIX[4] and the average execution size in our system. In other words, when the VIX is rising, the average execution size in block trading tends to decline because this volatility tends to scare off block volume. For those of you who don't know, we at Liquidnet have a 100 percent buy-side only community that trades directly with each other. Even in this buy-side to buy-side community, you as the buy-sider don't want to put up 250,000 shares in one trade. Rather, you'll put it up in pieces, say 50,000 shares, then 40,000, going back and forth all day until you get a sense of comfort about how to complete the entire block.

ALAN HILL: How the traders at buy-side institutions are measured is a little bit of the driver here. Jones, a little like Liquidnet, operates for buy-side to buy-side customers, trading natural blocks of liquidity. For example, we might handle a customer order for 300,000 shares in a stock that typically has an average daily volume of 50,000 shares. It is like customers being sometimes hung up on the VWAP[5] but then are afraid to spread out their orders in the marketplace at the same time. They are afraid of the potentially adverse impact on the performance of their orders. It will be interesting to hear what Matt has to say about that. We hear it all the time. On one side is an institutional customer who wants to get an order execution done, and on the other side of the trade is another institution. But why does this other institution not want to get the execution done with the first institution? What is happening here? Yes, I'm a little bit afraid.

LYONS: I agree. You can't divorce the advent of transaction cost analysis, which holds traders accountable to meeting specific benchmarks, from the effect of higher volatility when it comes to a reduction in the amount of blocks that have been traded.

---

[4] Ticker symbol for the Chicago Board Options Exchange (CBOE) Volatility Index. It tells the market's expectation of 30 day volatility.

[5] Volume Weighted Average Price

They go hand in hand. We've had other periods of higher volatility where blocks haven't dropped as much as they have recently. This needs to be looked at.

We have, intuitively, always thought at our shop that you don't want perverse incentives by putting in non-important benchmarks in an investment process on the trading desk to hamper the overall results that shareholders get. I am talking here about misapplying trading benchmarks to minimize transaction costs. That's when the goal of an actively managed investment firm is to maximize investments. Beating VWAP may not necessarily lead to better investment results per se.

SHAPIRO: We are all in violent agreement. That's our catchphrase at Tradebook! That is, we are all saying the same thing today. Let's talk about what Matt and Alan were saying about traders. The theory is this: as the buy-side kind of morphed into the sell-side, there was this view that the skill set of buy-side traders would rise. Buy-side traders out-sourced, generally speaking, in the past. That is to say, this previous generation of buy-side traders would sometimes take an order and hand it over to someone else to work, say to buy one million shares of IBM. In the old days, they'd call their sales trader at Goldman. Look how those times have changed. Today's buy-side trader possesses more skills and uses different electronic, direct access, and algorithm tools. In some cases, they have come over from the sell-side and they already know how to work the orders themselves. When you took that subset of trader and combined it with transaction cost analysis, or TCA[6] – which was really supposed to judge performance – it changed the risk profile of traders.

First of all, if you are able to buy blocks consistently at the low and sell consistently at the high then you are amazingly good as a trader, and it speaks to a different skill set. It does speak to the fact that you better be right, because 90 percent of institutions use TCA. Therefore, the idea of execution risk changing got traders to be less brave with regard to the sourcing of liquidity around large sizes.

In this sense, execution risk is no different than portfolio risk, but it is on the implementation side. You can argue that a lot of electronic Alternative Trading Systems, or ATSs, have an agency model. Agency trading tends to suffer during commission compression.[7] That might be more the cyclical side of it. In any event, you have essentially a secular dynamic, the irreversible decline in block trading, coinciding with this cyclical dynamic because of trading conditions due to economic and other factors such as a temporary reduction in volatility. It is creating pain for a lot of firms.

I remember being here at the Baruch Conference two or three years ago on a day when Liquidnet traded 80 million shares, a record at the time in transaction volume. The floor here at Baruch on that day was filled with New York Stock Exchange specialists, who were still talking about how their model worked. Not to insult the

---

[6] Transaction Cost Analysis is a detailed examination of the various costs of trade executions including the costs of buying or selling securities, spreads, commissions, market impact and other variables.

[7] For more recent perspective see, New levels of Transparency, The Trade USA, March 120, 2012 http://www.thetradenews.com/USA_Features/The_Big_Idea/New_levels_of_transparency.aspx

old model, but we said, "Hey, by the way, there is an ATS that traded 80 million shares today, so get real about what you do for a living!"

Let's talk now about transparency. Transparency is one of these incredibly vague nouns. But, it means a lot to people on this panel. When I say transparency, what is the first thing you think of?

LYONS: The fundamental needs of an institutional investor on the buy-side trading desk have not changed since I started on the buy-side 15 years ago. You need access to liquidity and the ability to contain information leakage. You need to assess the impact you are having in the marketplace so that you can adjust the strategy you employ to get that liquidity. That is where transparency comes in. In the old days, you could see your prints on the tape. You could understand the impact you were having, the imbalance of supply and demand you might be creating. In real time, you could then adjust your strategy.

That has been erased in today's market structure. You don't have the ability as a buy-side trader to react in real time. You rely on algorithmic strategies to do that for you. You try to do it more at the macro level by monitoring the overall impact of the algorithmic strategies you employ. That is, monitoring the sell-side fundamental performance is challenging when there is a lack of understanding, and transparency from the sell-side to the buy-side exactly as to where their orders are routed; why they are being executed where they are; and what are the underlying strategies they employ in their smart order routing technologies. Whenever this information is available, we have asked for it, so we can perform studies on the data. But, it certainly has not been the case that the brokers have been forthcoming to the buy-side in explaining how their routing is fulfilling their best execution obligations.

KONSTANCE: I hear it over and over again from clients. It is a tough commission environment. It is a very fragmented, complex market. What they don't want to see is their order being treated like a free option. They want to make sure that their orders are not adversely selected by trading against a much bigger size or something they shouldn't be trading against. They don't want to be in this kind of a toxic trading environment.

Also, they are concerned about their broker doing the right thing. For instance, is the broker preferencing venues correctly? This is a very tough issue and there are no clear rules. Brokers can be financially incented to use venues based on their economics. Depending on the circumstances, venue selection may make a difference in the client's quality of execution. You really have to be thinking about the ultimate transaction cost for the client, and not just for the broker.

Someone was telling me a story the other day. They saw their algorithms were trading 60 percent or more with one broker's dark pool of liquidity. No dark pool is bigger than two percent of the market, so you have to wonder if the algorithm was constructed to spend too much time in the dark and might be missing prints in lit markets.[8] If the broker is not doing the right thing, that will come out in the client's

[8] Lit markets are, in a sense, functionally opposite to dark markets. In lit markets, prices and trading data are publicly displayed prior to execution, which is not the case in dark markets, or "dark pools."

transaction-cost analysis. As a broker, you have to be thinking of how you satisfy your client in the long run. Otherwise, these little transitory gains will disappear with the client.

MARY McDERMOTT-HOLLAND: Is transaction-cost analysis measuring the right price? It is measuring execution price, implementation cost; it is measuring your impact cost. With so many orders taking place in the dark, is real price discovery or transparency there without publicly displayed liquidity? If more of that order flow were coming to a lit market, would there be better price discovery? Would there be lower transaction costs? I do not know the answer. This is not a commercial, but one of the reasons NASDAQ has introduced a US equity price-size market is that we believe trading should not be always about price time.[9]

For many years on the buy-side, we talked about what would happen in a price-size market. The institutions really are where the size comes from in trading. And so, if they were able to participate based on size, it would not be strictly about trading in milli-seconds anymore. It is not all about the speed. It is about size! It is about getting the portion of the trade that you're entitled to.

KONSTANCE: You know, Mary, I'd say that most players in the marketplace are good. I am not bashing high-frequency traders. They add a lot of value. And there are always nefarious actors everywhere. There is always somebody trying to trade against somebody somewhere. That's life. That happens in both dark and lit markets. There is a tremendous onus on us who are on the sell-side because we are entrusted with orders. We need to think about how to best construct an algorithm. We do spend a lot of time on anti-gaming and details such as, when we post an order, are we making it a free option? Are we giving away information? If we are not thinking about these issues all the time, our performance will suffer.

McDERMOTT-HOLLAND: I am certainly not talking about gaming. I am talking about true price discovery. Is it really happening in the dark? When you think about what we are talking about, the exchanges end up with the exhaust of all the orders after they have already been internalized at the Alternative Trading Systems, or ATSs. Then all of the dark systems are using the prices established at the exchanges. Is that real price discovery?

ESKANDAR: This is an age-old debate that I know is near and dear to Bob Schwartz's heart. We've spoken about call markets, price discovery, and quantity discovery. It ultimately goes back to the ultimate needs of the investor who is trying to execute an investment idea on behalf of shareholders.

Your initial question was about transparency. You can't get to a level of comfort with transparency unless you have standards. You take a look at the proliferation of ATSs, and even exchanges, broker models, routing logic and routing practices. I think that it is an obligation of any service provider to supply their customers, their

[9] NASDAQ OMS Launches First UD Equity Price-Size Exchange, *Globe Newswire*, September 20, 2010.

See, http://www.msnbc.msn.com/id/39264802/ns/business-press_releases/t/nasdaq-omx-launches-first-us-equity-price-size-exchange/#.T9IcLzVYvUg

members, with a detailed account of their practices. Where do they go? Who do they interact with? What are their incentives for routing the flow? By answering these questions, you are educating the end customer. Let the end customer then choose the partner he wants to trade with. That is on the transparency side.

The whole price discovery, quant discovery side is a really big debate that is probably bigger than this panel. I do believe that quant discovery is absolutely essential to the instructional investor needs. Without it you have 100 shares being traded when you need 100,000 shares traded. Trades of 100 shares in size doesn't help me very much.

SHAPIRO: Matt just reminded me of something we used to do at my previous employer, Morgan Stanley Investment Management. We very earnestly tried to get a lot of information from our trading counterparties – the brokers – about transparency. We had this mantra that we had to know more about how we trade than they know about how we trade.[10] We always felt that the really good sell-side shops knew us better than we knew ourselves. This made us feel a little insecure.

The truth is that you have two problems, two challenges. First, you have to ask the right questions to get an intelligent response rather than an obscure response. For example, if you ask the sell-side, "Do you send out IOIs[11] with my order"? The answer is, potentially, "No. My smart router does, we don't," and then you get into the semantics of the game. (laughter) A more interesting and confusing response might be, "We don't send out IOIs, we send out IOLs," What the hell is an IOL? It is an Indication of Liquidity; it is new, we have just created it.[12] It is kind of a game. I think that a lot of the sell-side firms do it. The buy-side, in an earnest attempt to fulfill their fiduciary responsibility, tries to keep up on these sorts of things.

Matt said to be careful what you wish for because you may just get it. That's meant to tell us that the buy-side is, quite frankly, still pretty lean. I don't know how many people are on your desk. Not everyone has a treasure chest of quants, and an unlimited number of programmers. If this information (for example, monthly transaction data, or a list of brokers who give you the best service, etc.) were to come into the house, where do you put it? Is it actionable? What do you do with it? It just resides in computer files in your in-box, and it is not actionable.

When I hear about transparency I think, yes, we can provide you with all this information. But what are you, or the trading desk, going to do with it when we give it to you? You never really get a good answer. Nevertheless, we are in the service business. We are all about providing that level of transparency to whoever wants it. I suppose that we could buy a storage bin somewhere locally to put all the hardcopy stuff in. More likely, the way the business is going, we could work with you in a consultative way to figure out how to actually take the data in and create the

[10] This explanation was provided on background only and should not be included as a footnote.

[11] IOI, or Indication of Interest, is an underwriting expression showing a conditional, non-binding interest in buying a security that is currently in registration (awaiting effectiveness by the SEC). The investor's broker is required to provide the investor with a preliminary prospectus. Source: Investopedia

[12] Seem It's Gray Out there, Nina Mehta, *Traders Magazine*, June 2008, http://www.tradersmagazine.com/issues/20_283/101171-1.html?zkPrintable=true

backend process, or product, that you need to solve whatever are your goals. That is probably where the evolution of that is going.

Trade reporting is another one of those topics where you can also go down the rabbit hole. You look at brochures and see ATSs advertising, "Our average block size is: whatever." Then there are two asterisks, two footnotes, and something else that directs you to some disclaimer about triple counting and adding stuff in to qualify this claim. How do we feel about that? Does that go to standards, Alfred, regarding trade reporting? Is that something we should be marching toward, doing a better job on?

ESKANDAR: That is a sensitive spot for us. We get frustrated the way some things are reported. We literally print our volume numbers daily. All our members get them. On good numbers we will high five each other; on bad days, we are not feeling so great. But, the execution numbers have been very consistent for ten years.

I see Justin Shack of Rosenblatt Securities in the audience. He does a great job tallying the different dark pools and reporting this in a consistent manner. It is frustrating because everybody wants to tout their numbers when they have done well. But, they don't want to give full disclosure on what they are actually doing. I don't believe that 10,000 shares of one executed stock trade is necessarily equivalent to 10,000 shares of another executed but different stock trade. For example, 10,000 shares of a highly-liquid Citi stock is not the same as 10,000 shares of some illiquid stock trade. There is obviously a difference in the difficulty involved in executing each order. If we can get to that granularity, to the point where we can actually show apples to apples comparisons, we can get a better idea of who is doing what.

SHAPIRO: Look at this battle cry for standards. Perhaps real-time venue reporting should be first on the list of these regulatory standards, which do not yet exist. Second should be some harmonization and agreed upon standards in which trade reporting would actually be presented and reported. Andy Silverman, the global co-head of electronic trading at Morgan Stanley, has really championed for some form of standard. Why are these cries for standardization coming from the sell-side and not from the buy-side? They are much less likely than the sell-side to lobby for this kind of change.

ESKANDAR: The answer is that the sell-side out-numbers Matt four to one right now on this panel! (laughter)

LYONS: I think the buy-side is generally concerned about real-time reporting, or creating opportunities to put something on the tape pointing to a large institutional order being in the marketplace. They are afraid that it will come back and cause front running for them. The printing of large blocks in real-time, especially when it involves the use of broker capital, alerts the market to imbalances in supply and demand.[13] I don't think that the buy-side has been concerned about making sure my prints are counted correctly. There is probably a problem with that. Transparency,

[13] The speaker subsequently explained in a follow-up interview how, in the instance outlined, there is a profit opportunity available for specialists to "free ride" off of the information obtained through the advertisement of the imbalance through the transaction printing to the tape.

liquidity discovery, size discovery: We, on the buy-side, want a little bit of our cake, and we want to eat it too. We want everyone else to show us what they have. But we don't want to show them what we have. Understandably so, because when you find that out the market liquidity tends to dry up quickly. The need for large block liquidity for a large asset manager is essential for us to implement portfolio decisions efficiently. Information on the availability of this liquidity helps us in this process.

However, there are a lot of smaller speculative investment firms that don't have the assets under management to respond to large block liquidity. But they can use the information to help them make an investment decision just based on imbalances in supply and demand. An active fundamental investor spends a large amount of resources making valuation judgments before an investment decision is made. A speculator trying to profit from supply demand imbalances, in effect, free rides off of this work.

McDERMOTT-HOLLAND: With the absence of a buy-side voice, the SEC makes a determination based on mostly sell-side input when they are taking a look at a consolidated audit trail and large trade reporting among other regulatory determinations.

LYONS: I sit on a number of industry committees and there is agreement – a consensus among the buy-side – that the consolidated trail and large trade reporting would be good additions to the framework that regulators work with.

McDERMOTT-HOLLAND: Yes, but the devil is in the details. Because, the question is, is large trade reporting real-time reporting?[14] I don't think that is what the buy-side wants. Is it end of day reporting? Is it once a week? The buy-side needs to be engaged in those debates with the regulators.

ESKANDAR: Rob, by standards, I don't mean real-time reporting. We as a firm and as a community for our members are aware that if you are utilizing an algo to trade say, one million shares and then reporting small pieces of that trade to the market, along with the identify of each trade, that will negatively work against the order. Reporting at the end of the trade day is one thing, but reporting these "child" orders intra-day is crazy.

SHAPIRO: The SEC is an amazing institution. They are now undertaking a four-year project on a consolidated audit trail that will cost an estimated two billion dollars.[15]

It is going to take a long time to create this consolidated audit trail. It will mean that, for the first time, you can keep track of what is going on in the marketplace in real-time. So, what are they doing now? The truth is that they are not doing anything. It is a little scary when you think about that from a systemic monitoring standpoint.

---

[14] McDermott-Holland in a follow-up interview distinguished between real-time report, which reveals a critical amount of trade data at an important stage in the trade cycle, and "real-time" trade reporting at the end of the day. That is an entirely different matter.

[15] SEC Proposes Consolidated Audit Trail System to Better Track Market Trades, *SEC Press Release*, May 26, 2010. http://www.sec.gov/news/press/2010/2010-86.htm

ROBERT LANG (Smarts Group, now NASDAQ OMX) From the Floor: In general, what is the difference between the regulatory needs of the buy-side versus the sell-side? Are they being met?

LYONS: I have worked with Ari Burstein, senior counsel in the securities regulation and capital markets group, of the Investment Company Institute (ICI).[16] He is one of the panelists at today's conference. Ari has represented the buy-side very well on the regulatory front, at least from our point of view. We like to work through the ICI a lot. The ICI represents a consensus view of a large group of players. Certainly, as discussed earlier, there are a lot of things that we think are shaking investor confidence, and these need to be addressed. As regards the needs of the buy-side, we must instill confidence back into the end investor, the retail customer, so that they aren't left with an uneasy feeling that the game is rigged. Ultimately, for markets to be more efficient, the more participants expressing their individual views on stock valuations through their investments the better. We believe the SEC understands most of the concerns of the buy-side in regards to perceived fairness, and they are taking steps to ensure that confidence can return. The consolidated audit trail, circuit breakers, and large trader reporting are a few of the steps we see as positive.

KONSTANCE: As a sell-side person, I believe the SEC is doing right by stabilizing the market. I don't see that your views would be a whole lot different than our views. Putting in circuit breakers and solidifying the rules for erroneous trades – these are things that unify the markets and prevent a Flash Crash. It is in everyone's interest. I don't see us lining up on opposite sides of the battlefield here.

HILL: Someone said this project, the consolidated audit trail, was started four years ago. So in 2006 they decided to build something that was going to be launched in 2010? That means they would have decided to build something when 90 percent of the market share was at the NYSE. Now the world has changed so much in four years that it is scary to think that we are going to pay for this. I don't know who will pay that four billion or one billion dollars a year. We are all going to be paying fees whether it is the buy-side, or the sell-side, or the consumer, with increased transaction costs. That is a little nerve-racking.

SHAPIRO: I always find it interesting when the SEC comes out with one of their pronouncements and opens it up for comments, there will inevitably be a conga-line of sell-side CEOs responding. Indeed, many of the CEOs represented here have gone up to Capitol Hill to testify. It is all part of public record. If called upon, Seth Merrin at Liquidnet would testify; ITG's Bob Gasser would testify. These are two examples of well-respected, knowledgeable industry leaders, and they have an agenda. They have something that they want to put into the statute that meets their business needs. In fact, Capitol Hill will invite the CEOs of various exchanges, ECNs, ATSs and even some of these high frequency firms, to testify.

Then the buy-side sends a letter via the ICI. That is a different interaction with Washington as it relates to the business of trading. It could very well be that the higher-ups at the investment management firms view trading as part of their

[16] The ICI is the national association representing US investment managers.

business, although not, of course, their entire business. Alan made a great point. Who knows in four years what sort of a market structure we'll have in place?

I was on a trading panel last night on the New York Stock Exchange. They were talking about the SEC's reaction to the May 6 Crash. One person said it reminded him of the Warren Report on the assassination of John F. Kennedy. That was a big document that explained away the event with some factual whatevers. But, does anyone really believe the explanation they gave? The resounding response was "no."

The SEC responded to May 6 by addressing the fear of the populous. So, if you are an individual investor, is it okay for May 6 to happen again? – God forbid, right?

So, for example, the market cannot trade more than 10 percent down under certain parameters.[17] They can now soften the blow of some systemic, cataclysmic event.

What the regulators did not really talk about was the greed side of May 6. That would have involved all of the high-frequency trading firms. The report did not provide a deeper understanding of what really occurred on May 6.[18] What were the high-frequency firms really doing? And what do we know about them? Around the time the report was published, there was a *60 Minutes* segment on CNBC about high- frequency trading.[19] It might be second nature to everyone in this room, but *60 Minutes* is known for doing a cool piece about something that most of America has no idea about. They will end it on a dramatic note that sends the hair standing up on the back of your neck. Then the segment goes, tick, tick, tick. That means that most of America now knows that high-frequency trading really exists.

The real take away is that they addressed the fear part, but they did not address the greed part. And, so I ask the question, what do we really know about high-frequency trading? How dangerous or how beneficial is it within our market structure? And what are we really going to do about it to protect the entire American trading apparatus from another systemic seizure?

HILL: From the perspective of our customers calling in – and Jones has only institutional customers – there is increased concern on the buy-side about whether

---

[17] The SEC and CFTC released a preliminary report on the flash crash incident on May 18, 2010. The report gave several working hypotheses, but failed to identify a single cause for the incident. Securities exchanges canceled 21,000 trades that were executed at unexpectedly low prices during the crash. On June 10, 2010, the SEC voted unanimously to enact new rules which automatically stop *trading* for any stock in the S&P 500 whose price changes by more than 10 % in any 5 min period. Source: Investopedia. http://www.investopedia.com/terms/f/flash-crash.asp#ixzz1zqXiQBGq

For a summary of more recent SEC regulatory action in this matter, see, Two Years After Flash Crash, SEC Still Pursuing New Safeguards, Michael Peltz, *Institutional Investor.*

http://www.institutionalinvestor.com/Article/3023836/Two-Years-After-Flash-Crash-SEC-Still-Pursuing-New-Safeguards.html

[18] Findings Regarding The Market Events of May 6th, 2010, September 30, 2010. See, http://www.sec.gov/news/studies/2010/marketevents-report.pdf

[19] See, Extra: How High Frequency Trading Grew. *60 Minutes*, CBS Newswww.cbsnews.com/video/watch/?id=6945166n

or not their orders are trading against high-frequency traders because trading against them could adversely impact their executions. This goes back to the transparency issue. At Jones, our business is the crossing of natural blocks of stock. Yes, there is a significantly increased buy-side concern on this matter of high-frequency trading hurting block executions.

LYONS: I would like to echo some sentiments made on the earlier panels. To lump high-frequency traders in one barrel is the wrong approach. It is not necessarily a bad thing that people are trading automatically. There are plenty of studies which show that the efficiencies of the market have been improved. There are other studies that show that there are some nefarious things occurring. These things include quote stuffing, flickering quotes, high cancellation to trade ratios, and information leakage in dark pools through flash orders and pinging. From the buy-side's prospective, those are the things that we worry about. It goes back to what I was talking about before – namely, the information content of my order flow is very valuable. My main concern is protecting that information during the implantation process so that the potential returns we expect are maximized.

McDERMOTT-HOLLAND: From NASDAQ's point of view, we look at the high-frequency firms as electronic market makers. As you said, there are good actors and bad actors. How you define a high-frequency trading firm is interesting. For instance, many of the large broker/dealers that the buy-side deals with have high-frequency trading arms too. As everybody said before, they can be your friend, or they can be your foe. It depends on how you are interacting with high-frequency trading firms.

KONSTANCE: We're definitely trading against them, just as we are trading against more traditional players. We don't know who is on the other side of a trade. High-frequency traders are 70 percent of the market.

McDERMOTT-HOLLAND: The argument is always that they are providing liquidity. Some on the buy-side say they are providing liquidity. It is hard to deny that spreads have compressed. Transaction costs have come down. But it is always healthy to take a look at practices in the market and to ask the important questions.

SHAPIRO: On a scale of one to ten with ten being perfect knowledge and understanding (and one being, "I have absolutely no idea how these folks are making money or how they are influencing the market place"), here is my question: Where do you think everyone in the room is, in terms of understanding, the effect – the impact, good or bad – of the interaction of high-frequency trading in our market system? Is it a 2 or 9, a 3 or 7? I can assure you it is closer to a one than a 10.

YURY MONAKOV (JP Morgan Asset Management) From the Floor: High-frequency traders do not make money on every trade. People assume that they are these toxic people who will always make money and pick you off. A lot of times you will pick them off because you have better information, you have better short-term alpha, you know things about your own order that they don't know. Come to the buy-side; know your stocks; know your portfolio manager; know more than what the high-frequency trader knows about his sector, about his stock, about the micro-structure. Keep up in a different way maybe.

SHAPIRO: I read you loud and clear.

LYONS: Yes, that is true. But what you don't know in every situation is if there are high-frequency traders who are looking for an informational advantage, to take an offsetting position. When an imbalance in supply and demand exists, high-frequency traders can take advantage of that, with little or no risk, by using the imbalance as basically a free option. If I know there is a large buyer out there, I can enter bids into the various exchanges knowing that at best I can buy in front of the large demand and offer it out at higher prices and, at worst, if the demand is not there, I am able to cancel my bids very rapidly. There is a high probability that a lot of the players are only looking for imbalances in supply and demand to trade profitably by free riding on the information. That is where it becomes problematic. Why? Because they have advantages in speed, co-location, low latency, speed and direct data feeds.[20] They take advantage of that. You just don't know enough about the inner workings of it to guard the alpha that you think you have in every situation.

KONSTANCE: It is really tricky. Reported ATS dark volume is 11 percent of total consolidated volume. And 60 percent of that 11 percent is with four firms.[21] Those four firms have a lot of high-frequency traders. I would not say that it is a negative. It is a challenge. High-frequency is a lot of things. It is market making. It is stat arb. It is not necessarily a bunch of evil-doers. In fact, I would say that the bad actors are just a tiny minority, but a minority nevertheless that you have to be aware of.

Maybe you are going to interact with them because there is liquidity out there. You should be smart about how you do it. It is like any other transaction. You can't go naively into it and say everybody has my best interest at heart. You have to understand the venue, and you must understand something about sizing the kinds of orders. If people want to turn off a venue that is always their right. Some people will. But I am not sure that we can always do that and continue to feel that we have all the sources of liquidity that are out there.

ESKANDAR: We polled our institutional members about their views on high-frequency trading, whether it is friend or foe, a positive or negative. You have groups that feel it is incredibly negative, that it does not add any ultimate benefit and value and does not help market efficiency. Then you get another group that says, I want the liquidity from high-frequency trading, I need the liquidity – and I don't care where the liquidity comes from. I trust that my portfolio manager has a better idea than the knucklehead who is trying to trade 200 shares in a milli-second in a high frequency marketplace. So, just give me that and help me complete my portfolio manager's wishes.

We discovered some people who would say, "Well, if a certain approach can protect them, then, yes, I do want to interact with this high frequency trading." If you as an investor can extract the benefit, then I guess it is not so bad for you. I really believe that a lot of it has to do with simple understanding and education. When the

---

[20] This refers to the ability of market participants to gain advantages in speed of trade execution through advanced technology, specifically the "co-location" of their computer servers near stock exchanges. That in turns lowers so-called latency, a critical factor in high-speed trade executions.

[21] In a study, Rosenblatt Securities attributed this 11 % of volume to Goldman Sach's SigmaX; Credit Suisse First Boston, Getco and Knight Capital Group.

end customer has that, and the optionality, to boot, it doesn't matter whether it is high-frequency trading or the next trend that comes along.

LYONS: In one respect, the jury is still out on the effectiveness of high-frequency trading. There has been a lot of discussion today about the ever-declining institutional impact costs that we have seen from ITG[22] other studies. Generally, the reported transaction costs have steadily declined from around 2004 to the present. The decline was interrupted starting in 2007, the beginning of the financial crisis and of heightened volatility. That's when you saw an uptick in institutional trading costs. It is being explained away at this point as a blip in volatility. It will be interesting to see now that volatility has come down. Will those costs also come down? In my opinion, it is not necessarily the case that the recent increase in trading costs are strictly a result of increased volatility. The increase in volatility coincided with Reg NMS[23] going into effect, and the New York Stock Exchange becoming electronic in 2007. And high-frequency trading soon took a majority share in equity volume at exchange. Correlation, of course, is not causality. I don't think we know yet what the ultimate effect high frequency trading has had on institutional impact costs.

JOE ROSEN (RKA Inc.) From the Floor: I am going to beat the horse and go back to the "F" word, "fragmentation." Is there a point where there are just too many venues to trade and that this is having a negative effect on the market? Not just the buy-side, but the market overall? If you do think there is a point, then what is that magic number? And please, let's not hear the same answer again, that "Yes, yes, we need competition!" I don't think that anyone will argue against having competition. Alfred, do you want to put your neck out?

ESKANDAR: Sure, I've got a long neck. Forty one, I think that is the current count.[24] It might go up to 50, and it might go down to 20, but who really cares? At the end of the day, you have a consolidated tape where every execution is printed. The institutional investor, and the retail guy – and my personal E*Trade account – have more sophisticated analytics than I even know how to use.

I don't have a problem getting access to pricing information. With all the connectivity and routing rules, everyone is connected to everyone. I don't think fragmentation is an issue. Ultimately, an order gets from one place to another, is executed, the print goes up, and it gets consolidated onto the tape. Everybody sees what the price is and continues to make their decision as to whether they want to continue to buy or sell.

Another question that we should probably ask is this: We have 1,600 broker/dealers. Is that too many? One thousand six hundred brokers! I don't get that. When we talk about too many ATSs, too many venues, there will be as many as the market

[22] Investment Technology Group.

[23] Regulation NMS, or National Market System, was enacted by the Securities and Exchange Commission in 2007 to foster competition among US exchanges and individual orders, and to promote fairness in price executions across all exchanges and platforms.

[24] *Bloomberg News* in January 2011 cited "more than" 40 dark pools, three ECNS and 13 stock exchanges operating in the US.

will bear. Ultimately, their value to the marketplace will either continue, or they will die off, or else be consolidated.

McDERMOTT-HOLLAND: You talk about dark pools; you talk about broker/dealers; you didn't talk about the fact that there are 13 exchanges today with the launch last Friday of BATS new exchange. It was 12 the week when NASDAQ launched its PSX exchange. For a long time, the barrier to becoming an exchange and obtaining a license as a self-regulatory organization was extremely high. It has become significantly easier over the past few years to become an exchange.

Is 13 exchanges the right number? I don't know. I don't know if 41 dark pools is the right number either. I actually thought it was 44. The natural market forces of competition will dictate the number. I remember years ago there were multiple ECNs, then there was consolidation among the ECNs. Natural forces dictate whether or not there is a need for all that exchange fragmentation. Now, for an exchange to be competitive, it needs to be innovative. It is not just about the pricing anymore. If you are going to introduce a new exchange, you have to introduce something that is truly new and different.

SHAPIRO: Are there too many blogs, too many electronic magazines, too many places you can buy? What about old-fashioned tube socks and lots of other stuff? If there is an unlimited venue to buy tube socks and other consumer stuff, why is there not an unlimited place to buy stocks? The Internet was basically able to aggregate information for the consumer. I'm not sure whether Google is comparable to a smart router. Still, my point is that if three years from now there are 172 different places to source liquidity, somebody is going to figure out an entrepreneurial solution to aggregating that liquidity. That is what is cool about this industry.

The ultimate consumer is everybody on this dais. We on the sell-side and the buy-side are consumers of liquidity. We have been provided a way to get our hands on that liquidity to accomplish our needs. Everyone has been predicting the consolidation of liquidity for as long as I've been in the business. Alfred's point is that 1,600 brokers are too many. I don't know if I have been hearing about the collapse of agency brokerage for as long as I have been in the business.[25] Every year there are more brokers. Every year there is a new way that enables brokers to come and do business.

Entrepreneurs have a way of figuring out these complexities more than anything else. I'd say that some of this has to do with technology. You can talk about all the dark venues and say that they will all be connected to a smart order router. But, when you have a smart order router, you have to get an acknowledgement to your order very fast. You have to get it within a few milli-seconds. If you have a very slow venue – and there are a lot of venues that are very slow – sometimes they are not even worth reaching. If it is going to take you 400 milli-seconds to get to it, even if they have liquidity, you can't get to it in any reasonable amount of time.

---

[25] In other words, as Robert Shapiro explained in a follow-up interview, the low barriers to entry have enabled a plethora of agency brokers to enter the market even though there had been no corresponding rise in trading volume. At times, in fact, there have been periodic declines in volumes.

So, technology will make a big difference as to who succeeds and who fails. The same thing applies to brokers. I see technology as this river – you have to jump in and keep going with it. You can't ever say you are against it, or against a change in it. You have to be investing like mad because it is moving so fast.

KONSTANCE: I was looking at smart order routers, and it was amazing what I saw the other day. There was an article about this guy who would see a quote and kept hitting his button but he was never getting the quote. He thought the reason was high-frequency traders jumping in front of him. What he didn't realize is, when he finally sees the quote, that it took 150 milli-seconds for that quote to get to him. That is the average quote time. To a high-frequency trader, a quote was visible in five microseconds and they reacted to that trade long before it was visible on a quote screen.

We all need to be invested in that technology that high-frequency traders use. I would not consider my institutional client base to be high-frequency traders. However, as a broker, we have had to put money into that kind of technology for institutional clients, so that when you see a quote, or we see a quote, we can act on it.

McDERMOTT-HOLLAND: Over the nearly 30 years that I have been in this business, I would argue that there has been a dramatic shift in the way the buy-side is being serviced. When I was on the buy-side, I had brokers calling us with stock lists – and technology made it more efficient. At what point are we getting to the edge of that technology where it is no longer a benefit but a detriment? Many of the brokers have merged. There used to be position trading desks and sales trading desks. There used to be over the counter desks and listed desks. Today, things are very different. Market participants have had to be nimble and have had to recreate themselves based on market forces. I think we will see that continue.

BILL HARTS (Harts & Company) From the Floor: I want to pursue the point that there are too many brokers. It sure seems like there are. Some even sent in sell orders on May 6 to sell Accenture for a penny. When it was down from over $40 a share. If my broker sold my Accenture stock for a penny, I'd find a different broker pretty fast. Marie, do you think that any of your portfolio managers would mind their orders waiting for 200 milli-seconds more, or for 400 milli-seconds more, if it meant that they might find more size, or a better price? Why is 400 milli-seconds such a horrible wait?

KONSTANCE: It is horrible because they are looking in the past. They are looking at something that doesn't exist anymore. By the time they see it, the trade has probably been executed.

LYONS: The question is, do we as a fundamental, active investor care about speed that much? I guess not. We are a long-term investor. We look for ideas that we hope will generate returns to our shareholders over a period of two or three years. We have a three to four year holding period. On the trading desk, when we are implementing those decisions, we need to compete with everyone else in the marketplace. In that sense, yes, we need the capabilities that the brokers provide to us to compete with the high-frequency traders. That is what we rely on. In the context of the needs of the buy-side to compete with high frequency traders, I am trying to stress that certainly our investment objectives are completely different. We have holding periods of years and HFT firms have holding periods of seconds. But, we do need access to the technology that is used in the market to efficiently interact with all types of available liquidity.

We rely on the brokers that do business with us to come equipped with the same co-located computers and the same low-latency smart order routing capabilities that the high-frequency traders have. That is what we ask them to provide to us and, for the most part, we get that. Would it be great to go back to eighths and quarters when the US markets traded in fractional amount and see 50,000 up and just go grab it? I guess so. But if you think about it, that is 120 basis points versus my ability to get stuff done now on the floor or on exchanges for 10 basis points. There is give and take in everything. I don't think you should think of these things in a vacuum.[26]

C.F. LEE (Rutgers University) From the Floor: I wonder if high-frequency trading will change or not?

O'BRIEN (Direct Edge) From the Floor: Michael Pagano at Villanova University postulates that the notion of liquidity that has largely been left out of the discussion is part of your fundamental curriculum. That brings us to where we are, that available liquidity can enable you to construct the perfect portfolio.

What we are really talking about is the sourcing of liquidity, and the various players within the context of liquidity. Execution risk, which is another variant of risk within the context of a large investment management company, is often overlooked as being something that is very germane to the investment management process. I assure you that if, God forbid, something calamitous happened in the world and Matt was called upon to start liquidating positions, but he was unable to do so, the notion of execution risk as it relates to liquidity would very quickly be clearly on his mind. People would start looking at executing venues as being really important to the entire investment management process.

There are only a few universities that I know of that has trading as a legitimate curriculum subject, and that treats trading as a legitimate skill. Baruch College is one of them. I would widely argue that it is still regarded as the red-headed stepchild at a lot of investment management firms. But it is an incredibly important function for lots of reasons, many of which we are talking about here. I stress: a great idea implemented poorly becomes a mediocre idea.

LYONS: To that end, is high-frequency trading affecting the ability to get the portfolio returns you expected from fundamental analysis? Investors who are looking to take advantage of supply and demand imbalances in the marketplace have existed since I started in the 80's. It has always been the same. Someone is always looking for a large order imbalance to take advantage of, and to position themselves in front of, to reap short-term profits.

Today, it is the players who have changed. The game has gotten a lot faster. Back in the day, the buy-side had been squawking about the specialist getting in front of

---

[26] Lyons elaborated further in a subsequent interview, adding: "I am agreeing that some of the issues that have the buy-side concerned are definitely perceptual in nature. In some sense the perception that liquidity was [once] more readily available was the fact that you could see it and access it. However, there was a cost to that in higher spreads."

them and the SOES bandit[27] getting in front of them. It is always the same thing and, to an extent, this kind of behavior will never be eliminated. To a certain extent, you need speculators to grease the wheels and provide liquidity.

JAMES ANGEL (Georgetown University) From the Floor: I have heard a lot of grumbling about there being too much fragmentation, too many markets. But I have never really understood what damage occurs because of it. If there are too many markets, what if anything should be done about that, and who should decide this?

LYONS: As long as you have access to liquidity, I don't think it is fundamentally a problem. Because of fragmentation there is this latency arbitrage ability for people to layer order books with liquidity that they don't plan to execute. They use the ability to quickly cancel residing liquidity on order books when they get a signal from an institutional order coming crossing the spread.

That is where the problems arise. The basic strategy is this: Layer the order book with bids and offers trying to determine where imbalances in supply and demand exist due to a large institutional order. There is low risk in this because you are paid a rebate to "provide" liquidity. Therefore, if you end up with a position, you can trade out of the position very quickly and at a penny spread and still capture a rebate even though you lose the spread. Conversely, if you can detect an institutional order, you can quickly cancel the balance of existing orders on the book and accumulate a position in front of the institutional order, taking advantage of the optionality of that latent supply and demand. At the same time, you hope to profit from that information gained through the free rider effect. I think it is a problem with the network. I think it is a growing problem. It is in its infancy and will probably reduce as time goes on.

ROSEN: I go back to a comment about the complexity of the network. I am not anti-competition. But, to compare how many places you can go buy socks to how many places you can trade stocks raises the issue of why this is a highly-regulated market. If there is too much regulation – that is a separate question. I personally think there is. But, it is a different question compared with asking, if there are 5,000 places to trade stocks, would that be too much? Sure, I would say yes. But is 50 too much? I don't know the answer, but 5,000 is too much.

Because of this complexity and the law of unintended consequences, things can go wrong, especially when you are trading in nano-second speed. I think it is too much for human regulators to deal with in terms of 5,000 places.

BERNARD DONEFER (Baruch College) From the Floor: In the past, the NASD's ACT[28] system had a 90-second reporting window. OATS, the Order Audit Trail System, was introduced to report and monitor trades. Then a three-second

[27] This was the slang term used to describe traders who used the Small Order Execution System introduced by NASDAQ in the wake of the 1987 market crash. SOES was introduced in response to complaints that NASDAQ market makers were not "picking up their phones" to take customer orders during the crash. SOES, however, became controversial since some market participants, notable NASDAQ market makers, accused users of SOES – the SOES bandits – of unfairly profiting at the expense of market makers. Markets makers complained that SOES bandits would make quick profits in the changes in the bid-ask stock price spread at times when the markets makers did not have enough time to update their quotes in fast moving markets.

[28] Automated Confirmation Transaction system.

reporting window was introduced. Now the SEC wants a real-time reporting system. Yet we are trading right now at speeds of 10 microseconds or less, with transactions and updates that are ever faster. Do you think the system can actually work so that the SEC will be able to keep everything in order? Will everybody's clock on everybody's computer, in every brokerage house, every buy-side trading desk, and every exchange be exactly dead on and synchronized? Will they be able to put together the audit trail they are expecting for four billion dollars plus two billion a year, plus tax, plus tip? (Laughter)

O'BRIEN: The answer is no.

McDERMOTT-HOLLAND: I don't think they said it was going to be real-time. That was a question asked in the SEC market structure Concept Release.[29] The SEC is looking for comments from the industry. So, should it be real time or is some other metric better?

HILL: In normal functioning markets, not stressed markets, it may be feasible. When there is a problem, it will not be feasible. There will be way too much activity. We saw this in the Flash Crash. Everyone was sitting at their desks with no idea of whether the quotes we were looking at were real.

O'BRIEN: No one cares unless the six sigma event[30] hits the fan, but then everyone wants to know why it happened. Unless you have that facility you can't get to it.

HILL: And everyone thinks it is working fine until the six sigma event happens.

McDERMOTT-HOLLAND: You don't think OATS is the right reporting mechanism for the consolidated audit trail? (Laughter)

SCHWARTZ: There has always been a natural tendency for these markets to consolidate. This tendency has always been there because there are natural economies of scale in market making. I would like to bring in that concept, and also the concept of price discovery.

Now we are seeing this fragmentation. I wonder if there had been a change given the regulatory environment and the technology environment that has somehow undercut the economics of scale. If it has, we might not ever see a re-consolidation.

LYONS: But did they exist before?

SCHWARTZ: I think they were always there.

O'BRIEN: The concentration of global liquidity was artificially constrained by the exchange mechanism, which set up bricks and mortar and gasoline fueled moats around their market share. It was never allowed to evolve in some capitalistic way, and this is what we have. I would like to go back to the point about Google. If Google is able to consolidate my ability to shop between 500 different websites to buy tube socks, I don't see why a smart router or some other entrepreneurial EMS front end can't consolidate 5,000 different port sources of liquidity.

---

[29] SEC Issues Concept Release Seeking Comment on Structure of Equity Markets, January 13, 2010. http://www.sec.gov/news/press/2010/2010-8.htm

[30] A six sigma event is defined as a price drop of six times the volatility (or standard deviations) of an asset.

HILL: The needs of the buy-side are incredibly diverse, which is why there are a lot of exchanges and venues. Lots of buy-side participants probably never interact in BATS or BIDS[31] or wherever else, but that's their choice. Someone's coming to Jones or Liquidnet for a similar reason. But that is going to be completely different than why they'd use execution services at Nomura, for example

SCHWARTZ: I suggest that for the next 25 minutes we fragment. (laughter) Then we can come back for the final session. Thanks, panel!

(APPLAUSE)

[31] BATS, for Block Interest Discovery Services, is a US-based ATS launched in 2006. BIDS, for Better Alternative Trading System, was launched in the US as an ECN in 2005 and is the operator of two stock exchanges in the US.

Chapter 5
New Technology: What Does It Bring to the Table?

Moderator: Marcus Hooper, *Pipeline Financial Group Ltd.*
Stuart Adams, *FIX Protocol Ltd.*
Paul Britton, *Capstone Holdings Group*
Joseph Cangemi, *ConvergEx*
Jim Ross, *Financial Markets Horizons*
Justin Schack, *Rosenblatt Securities, Inc.*
Joseph Wald, *Knight Direct LLC*

ROBERT SCHWARTZ: It is my pleasure to introduce our moderator, Marcus Hooper. I can't think of another moderator or speaker here today I have had more beers with than Marcus. (Laughter)

MARCUS HOOPER: I should qualify that Bob. It was all in the interest of liquidity. (Laughter) The breadth on this panel is extraordinary. I would not be surprised if it has 150 years of collective experience.

Bob Schwartz said he was thinking of four measures: You referred to the markets providing important services in terms of facilitation of the transfer of capital; the discovery of quantity which is something we often don't talk about; price discovery; and, finally, encouraging the issuance and creation of capital to get people coming to the markets. Based on those four measures of market quality, has technology been a success or a failure?

JOSEPH CANGEMI: As noted, I have been in the business for about 150 years! (laughter). I have experience with all market models, from a physical floor market to a worldwide company today. I spent 25 years at the New York Stock Exchange. Today, I am an electronic project manager of sales and trading in some 50 markets for BNY ConvergEx. In all cases, it is the same customer, the same investment needs, and the same obligations insofar as customer expectations for service and executions are concerned. And it is the same solutions that I need to provide on a different playing field, or execution environment. The company I am partnered with created a tool set that allows customers to basically do the same things they were asking me to do for them 25 years ago – but in a different environment. I would say that technology has been very successful in providing the exact resource it set out to provide, in the process creating this evolving market structure today which has replaced the former market that was dependent on a centralized physical floor location. Now is any market perfect? No, and I guess we will get into that discussion today.

R.A. Schwartz et al. (eds.), *The Quality of Our Financial Markets: Taking Stock of Where We Stand*, Zicklin School of Business Financial Markets Series,
DOI 10.1007/978-1-4614-5592-9_5, © Springer Science+Business Media New York 2013

JIM ROSS: Technology has brought more efficiency. It has helped to bring investors, brokers and exchanges closer together. We have a tendency to generalize about technology, much as we do about transparency. In many ways, the past several decades, generally speaking (certainly the 80's, 90's and 2000's) have seen the efficiencies play out. That, however, is different than market innovation. While we have seen the great benefits of the efficiencies, we are now starting to wrestle with quality. And that goes back to the theme of this conference. What is the element of quality that is in price discovery, in quantity discovery, in capital formation? We often joke about the unintended consequences of regulation. There are unintended consequences of technology too. Certainly we have talked about fragmentation, the impact on price discovery, and other things like that.

Look at how technology has played out and, ultimately, look where it is going on the market structure front. In the 1980's and 90's, I was running the crossing network at Instinet.[1] Then all of a sudden the New York Stock Exchange came out with its own after-hours crossing network. I thought, that is it. We are done! How are we going to compete against the exchange? Well, obviously, I later ended up joining the New York to introduce a new crossing network there.[2] I had always felt that the exchange would provide the final solution to the challenges of technology. But I have changed my tune in the past several years. We have a much different dynamic now. Our market structure is not necessarily going to be an exchange-based environment.

STUART ADAMS: Like Jim, my formative years were spent at Instinet, but on the other side of the pond in London. I spent a lot of time in airplanes flying back and forth. Technology now means that much more is being done remotely. That's also the case with people who are seeking capital. Clearly, you have a more globalized market in today's technologically advanced environment. People can access capital markets around the world because of technology. I now miss having beers with Marcus because we don't need to travel to the same places anymore (laughter).

Technology is still very evolutionary, not revolutionary. How do things move on from a latency perspective?[3] How fast is too fast? How does regulation keep pace with technology? There are many more topics that still need to come forward. I spend more time now on the FIX protocol.[4] I am not talking about how to buy and

[1] Instinet, launched in 1967 as Institutional Networks Corp. and offering trading in anonymity for institutional investors, is regarded as an early and ground-breaking electronic pioneer.

[2] This crossing network was created in 2005 with Ross as a founding partner. It was sold to the NYSE and launched as NYSE MatchPoint in 2006 with Ross joining as vice president of the business.

[3] Latency measures the length of time to execute a trade from order entry to execution. The speaker is referring to the ability of market participants to gain advantages in speed of trade execution through advanced technology, specifically the "co-location" of their computer servers near stock exchanges. Lower latency is generally driven in proportion to the nearness of the servers to the exchanges.

[4] The Financial Information Exchange (FIX) protocol is the messaging standard for pre-trade and trade communication in the global *equity markets*.

sell shares, but with regulators around the world who are talking about the impact of standards, technology and regulation.

PAUL BRITTON: We are experiencing a paradigm shift. Fundamentally, Professor Schwartz is always talking about markets being used as a transfer mechanism for risk. In my view, right now, you are seeing an enormous transfer of risk from the typical sell-side institutions to the buy-side because of regulation and Dodd-Franks.[5] The sell-side has been forced by the regulators and regulations to deleverage to reduce the size of their risk on their balance sheets. Technology will play a key role in that transfer to the new risk warehouse, that is, to somewhere on the buy-side. Where exactly is the new risk warehouse?

I am biased. I run a hedge fund, so I am hoping that it ends up being in a hedge fund world. I had better make sure that my technology is very, very robust. Because regulation is forcing the use of more technology in the regulation of capital markets, exchanges will play a greater role in providing transparency either for the regulators or for the capital markets. Regulators are pushing for more transparency in our markets. That is a very positive development, because centrally cleared houses or exchanges will house a lot of this risk. Technology will play an absolutely critical part in making sure this is facilitated efficiently.

JUSTIN SCHACK: You can separate the increased use of technology in financial markets, particularly the stock market, from the way market structure has transformed. I look at them in tandem. Today's market structure, being almost entirely automated, is very fast and very efficient. I compare this with the market structure that prevailed before technology became more prevalent. It is very difficult to argue that technology has not been tremendously beneficial. If you look at the transaction costs analysis, if you look at spreads, if you look at the outcomes on both the institutional and the retail investor side, they are dramatically better. People used to trade Intel for a ¼ spread. That was back in the 90's, when the old market makers were colluding to not quote in odd eights.[6]

Today you are trading Intel for a penny, or you are trading Citi for a penny. The real spread in Citi is much less than a penny.[7] There have been a lot of comments today about how we are struggling with some of the imperfections in the market. And there are some imperfections. On the whole, though, technology has been a very powerful force for good in the financial markets.

JOSEPH WALD: No question. Many sell-side people talk about the regulatory environment as something that is challenging and difficult, and that presents a lot of

---

[5] The Dodd–Frank Wall Street Reform and Consumer Protection Act (Dodd-Franks) was signed into law by *President Obama* on July 21, 2010.

[6] NASDAQ market makers were accused in the late 1980s of abusing their privileges by not providing liquidity and two-sided continuous quotes at the time of the 1987 market crash. That led to the introduction of the Small Order Execution System (SOES). More significantly, these same market makers were also accused of colluding to keep bid ask spreads on stock prices artificially wide, a practice characterized by only quoting stocks in even one eight increments (i.e., 0, 2/8, 4/8, 6/8).

[7] Schack said in a follow-up interview that investors would be willing to quote Citi in increments of less than a penny if the minimum increment was lowered from a penny.

unknowns. It is to the regulators' credit that we have the marketplace that we have today. If it wasn't for the Crash in '87 and the subsequent SOES mandate[8] allowing electronic trading and technology to actually have a place in this market structure, we would never be where we are today. In many respects, the regulators deserve a tremendous amount of credit with respect to bringing the implementation of technology into the marketplace.

A lot of what we will talk about over the next year is this: How this new regulatory environment will once again create opportunities for technology to really take hold and create a new marketplace for us. For example, being able to leverage the potential new regulatory environment to create opportunities and to do things that are innovative such as a new strategy or a new business model.

HOOPER: It strikes me that technology is being used in different ways by different people. Is technology actually now getting to a point where it is a fundamental barrier to entry for certain users of the marketplace?

ADAMS: It could be seen as a very unfair playing field to those participants who can't afford certain trading technologies to compete with other participants with deep pockets who can afford this same technology. On the other hand, affordable technology can level the playing field for all participants. The real way a normalization of that imbalance can happen is clearly to make sure that there is a level playing field through the use of standards, such as the FIX Protocol. Standards have always been seen as this really boring thing behind the scenes. But really they are a fundamental part of our people and their business planning. If we want to go into a new business, what standards will be at play? How do bodies such as the ISITC[9], which represent these standards, work together across the industry? Do we have interoperability between standards?

In the European sense, we have learned an awful lot from what has happened in the US. Indeed, I spent the best part of 20 years in this industry introducing several American financial technology companies and their services to the European investment community. I learned from the experiences. We can also learn a lot in Europe today from the US from the perspectives of both a consolidated tape in the US and the post-trade side since there is no industry-wide consolidated tape in Europe. First, there is no structure in place in Europe. Second, the standards underlying it are not there.

Today, CESR[10] published a document referring to the use of non-proprietary protocols and open standards. A lot of that concern about an unfair playing field starts to fade as we move as an industry to non-proprietary protocols and open standards. It won't happen overnight, but you end up with an environment that allows people

---

[8] Small Order Execution System introduced in response to the 1987 Crash. Market makers attracted criticism for not "picking up their phones" to take customer orders.

[9] The International Securities Association for Institutional Trade Communication (ISITC) was founded in 1991 by financial industry leaders and competitors who saw the benefit of facilitating straight-through processing (STP) among custodian banks, investment manager, and broker *dealers*. Source: ISITC Website, http://www.isitc.org/history.cfm.

[10] The Committee of European Securities Regulators. It is an independent EU Authority in the securities markets.

to innovate from a more level playing field. On the consolidated tape issue in Europe, it reminds us that, as regards innovative approaches to market structure, there is often an initial reluctance from the likes of the data vendors to make the corresponding technological adjustments in standards. Somebody has to change something to move forward as an industry. There is often a hesitation among participants to take the first steps! Eventually, however, market participants come around to accepting that the changes are good for their business models. They ultimately recognize the opportunities to differentiate themselves again.

BRITTON: The reason I came over to the US ten years ago was to open up a North American branch of Mako Global Derivatives.[11] We were option market makers. I came to compete in the US options markets on the International Securities Exchange and on other options exchanges. I invested in the servers and technology. But within three months they were outdated because of advances in the speed of executions and latency! My traders would scream at me that they could not compete. Ken Griffin at Citadel[12] has just bought the new super duper Sun Servers 4500 which cost $10 million and we were only using Sun Server 3500, which cost $500,000! I realized that technology was becoming a barrier to entry for me, that I just couldn't afford it. Fast forward to today. Technology has enabled us to get back into the marketplace. In my eyes, it is a much more level playing field just from a cost perspective. In the old days, whoever spent the most amount of money won. It was a technology arms race in that sense. But it was a tough business model to follow. Today, it feels as though technology, just from a hardware prospective, has become commoditized. Now I have a simple answer whenever I hear the technologists or traders shouting that Citadel's server is only three millimeters away from the exchange server, but we are four millimeters away from the exchange server so how the hell can we make money? I say that, if it is down to one millimeter, we shouldn't be competing in this market. Ten years ago, I made the decision that the barrier to what we could capture from the revenue standpoint through investment technology just wasn't worth it. Now, because the hardware is commoditized, and with the decline in technology costs, it has become a more level playing field. It was much more expensive in the past.

SCHACK: One of the things lost in this debate is often from a market structure and fairness perspective. The question is asked, "Does Aunt Minnie in Kansas need to have co-location when she is trading through TD Ameritrade?" Do institutional investors need to have co-location? It has already been said, but it is worth repeating: There are brokers who will make sure that they are co-located so that you – the retail and institutional investor – don't have to make that investment on your own and spend the money to have the same technology as the high-frequency market makers. A lot of the brokers do that now. Pretty much all the big institutional brokers that have algorithms and dark pools are taking advantage of the same co-location services.

[11] Mako Global Derivatives is part of London-based Mako Group operating since 1999 and active in the equity, fixed income and commodity options markets.

[12] Ken Griffin is the American hedge fund manager. He is the founder and CEO of Citadel LLC, a Chicago-based investment firm launched in 1990.

On the exchange side, the providers of co-location services are doing everything they can in the wake of the crisis to make sure that access is fair and pricing is fair. I am not just talking about the exchanges but about other providers as well. A one millimeter co-location 'advantage' doesn't actually matter because that tech hub out in Mahwah, NJ that is offering co-location services is making sure that its customers can compete technologically on a level playing field with someone who is one millimeter nearer to an exchange. So, I don't think that technology is a significant barrier to entry. There are folks who will invest in it because it fits their business model. Then there are folks who won't invest in it but who can take advantage of intermediaries in the market that have made that investment.

ROSS: Once we get over the efficiencies of technology and digest that into our marketplace, the question becomes, are we innovating in that disruptive technology in a way that enables us to do something differently than before? Not more efficiently, but actually different? It is really important to remember when we talk about the barriers to entry, that technology has enabled new ideas to emerge. These could be ideas about approaches to either price discovery, liquidity discovery, or even cross asset trading. I am not actually that impressed with our passionate pursuit of latency. Yes, I see that very linear, faster, faster, and faster aspect to it. That's fine. But how does it really affect market quality? How is it really helping? It has brought some innovation on the high-frequency front for sure. But, ultimately, I wonder if that was quite the paradigm shift I was thinking about. How fast can we get?

I was talking earlier with Keith Ross[13] about this. I said alright, let's get as fast as we need to so that we can start looking at different market models and innovations that rethink how we aggregate liquidity, how we come to price discovery. One thing about being a Bob Schwartz fan is that the call auction is how we can think about integrating some of this stuff. The potential benefits for call auction trading in our markets has not gotten the attention it has deserved over the decades. It has been a limp adjunct to the price discovery world and to the continuous world. Yet we have seen where brief pauses during difficult trading periods can sometimes make a positive difference.

CANGEMI: If a customer has a need, someone will develop an answer or solution and provide it at a value. That is inherently what competition in our industry is about. Three or four years ago, the competition was centered on speed. We have never really talked about this before: Our industry has always been focused on reducing the time and distance between the ultimate investor and the point of sale. The numbers cited in the reduction of time for the execution of a trade today may sound incomprehensible to the normal person. Let's go back to the panel before, where they were speaking of the frustration of that gentleman who couldn't access that bid every time he saw it and pushed a button. That is probably not the way you want to trade in this environment. If the investor has a price point, an idea or a concept, and the technology from a broker, they will have order types that will allow you to execute that idea in this market structure. An investor today must learn to use

[13] Keith Ross is CEO of alternative trading system PDQ Enterprises.

today's execution order types to accomplish their investment goals. The markets are too fast to interact with manually. You are competing with other investors who have adapted these order types and are utilizing their data processing capabilities. But to say that you want to do it the way it was done ten years ago in today's market structure is irresponsible.

To expect regulation to come to your rescue and either revert the structure of the markets back to what they were, or to say that the way you executed orders ten years ago is the way you should be allowed to do it today, would be protectionist and inefficient. Competition is the key. I agree that standards in our industry have always been something we are striving for, and we will continue to strive for them. There are lists of information that need to be standardized. We are currently talking about a lot of initiatives from a regulatory standpoint that need some standards behind them. The SEC and FINRA must work with the industry to establish a consolidated audit trail and requirements for large trader reporting.[14] Each would provide for proper surveillance across all markets and for a more efficient means for the industry to research market events like those of May 6.

The previous buy-side panel talked about what data they wanted from a broker. Not one of them had the same set of requirements. Many of my institutional clients have asked for execution data sets yet none have really figured out how to utilize it. This idea of standardized data is a very big part of the competitive landscape between brokers right now. The broker or consortium of brokers that can find the solution inevitably will make this marketplace stronger and better. It is not a barrier; it is actually the catalyst to make this market more efficient.

WALD: Technology is about much more than speed. We are already approaching the point where we won't be able to go much faster. We are in a micro-second world. That is about as fast as it can get when it comes to the speed of light. So, from that perspective, the easy one from a technological solution was to become faster. Whoever had the opportunity will continue to get there, but eventually that will be a level playing field because now all market participants can effectively achieve speed with the right resources. The real innovation, the real excitement with technology, is on its way now. Because, if you have a level playing field how do you differentiate yourself? That is where the entrepreneurial spirit and innovation take hold. People will start to talk about what they can do about sourcing liquidity in a more effective way.

What can I do about creating a different market structure that helps implement my trading idea? What can I do to help minimize information leakage? What can I do to continue to find the right counterparty to trade with? Those are the exciting parts of where we are today in the evolution of the markets. The speed game definitely matters for a lot of participants. But, at a certain point (and that point is coming very quickly) we will be there. After all, there is a finite point in how fast

[14] Rick (Richard) Ketchum, Chairman & CEO, FINRA, discussed this in his testimony before the Subcommittee on Securities, Insurance, and Investment Committee on Banking, Housing, and Urban Affairs United States Senate, May 20, 2010. See, http://www.finra.org/Newsroom/Speeches/Ketchum/P121509

you can go! Everyone will be able to trade as fast as they want, whether it is the retail trader, the institutional trader, or the high-frequency trader. Everyone will have that type of access to low latency and speed of executions.

HOOPER: It sounds like the panel is almost agreeing that we are already too fast?

WALD: I wouldn't say that we are too fast. I am saying that we will be as fast as it can get and that is not too fast. That is the right speed.

HOOPER: Let me be the cynic. When we get to that point, there will be some people who will just be better, some people will have their cables a couple of millimeters shorter than the next guy, and it will actually make a difference. Will we end up in the situation where, at a certain level of trading, there will be just the haves and the have not's? Is that likely?

WALD: I don't think so. Low-latency technology is open to anyone who is willing to make the investment.

CANGEMI: It is really simple. I spent 25 years on the floor of the NYSE repositioning myself around the trading floor until I was in the most effective location for providing execution services to my customers. As their needs changed over time, I changed my location to match those needs. I was effective and efficient. It's the same thing with today's technologies. We have co-located our execution engines to better position ourselves to provide those execution services to the same customer. How long is someone going to be faster? I am not sure. Is the time and speed advantage for only a weekend today, compared with, say, a year in the past? In other words, is this speed advantage now much shorter lived?

I don't know. It is a relevant issue that someone is faster than me, and that my customer needs me to be faster and cheaper. I have to find a way to do that for my customer, otherwise I become disposable. That is not the nature of our business.

JIM ANGEL (Georgetown University) From the Floor: We need to draw a distinction between two types of speed. One is the race between investors to get to an order that is sitting there. That race has been going on for 400 years. There is nothing wrong with it, and nobody will stop it. If there is a good order sitting there, it is just a race, and the first one there gets it. The real concern is the market participants reacting to each other so fast that it will create a positive feedback loop that will destabilize the market. What is your thinking on that second type of speed. Is it a problem? And, if it is, what if anything should we do about it?

SCHACK: This is one of the issues that we are all grappling with right now within this context of a much more efficient market structure that is delivering better outcomes for people because of technology. It is clear that the market has lacked sufficient and coordinated mechanisms to slow trading down, and to interject some form of human judgment in an event like May. That's when we need to slow down the process and figure out why markets are going down, and to determine how to re-inject some liquidity into the markets. This has been covered on previous panels. Yes, the SEC acted pretty quickly to get circuit breakers in place. In this context, we are talking about going to a better coordination across markets. These things are appropriate.

ANGEL: Of course, one could say that, on May 6, the markets were not fast enough, that the data integrity problems indicated that the market data feeds could not keep up with the flow of activity. So, you can spin May 6 the other way – that our markets weren't fast enough to keep up with the flow of activity.

BRITTON: I disagree with Justin on May 6. I don't think anything went wrong.

ANDY BROOKS (T. Rowe Price) From the Floor: You don't think the trading was wrong in Accenture on May 6? When somebody routed away from a lot of markets to get Accenture temporarily down to a penny a share from $41.00 a share?

BRITTON: Yes, I saw those trades.

BROOKS: I'm in Topeka. I tell my broker to sell one thousand shares of Accenture. In six minutes it trades down to one penny. And something is not wrong? That is best execution, that is order flow routing? That is, wow, really?

BRITTON: If someone wants to sell 75,000 futures, they have every entitlement to sell 75,000 futures. It is a free market system where every investor and market participant should make their own determination. If Accenture is trading at a penny, and you want to sell it at that, that is your problem – it is a free capital market. I don't think it is the regulator's responsibility to step in. If a guy wants to sell 75,000 futures he should have the right and the ability to be able to do that.[15]

ANDY BROOKS: I agree.

BRITTON: Now, if they decide to sell them in three minutes, that is going to cause huge implications in the marketplace. I was expecting the fat finger on May 6 to be the issue, but it wasn't.[16] I thought the problem occurred after somebody wanted to sell 75 futures and instead erroneously entered 75,000. In actual fact, it was a legitimate order – somebody legitimately wanted to sell 75,000. It wasn't a fat finger. It was intentional as it later emerged. They should be allowed to do that.

BROOKS: Even if they put the entire market at risk?

BRITTON: That is their decision. It is a free market.

BROOKS: I like to go one hundred miles an hour through a school zone. That is dangerous, that is reckless.

BRITTON: Right.

BROOKS: If their order or someone's order is like that, is that not reckless?

BRITTON: If that is what they want to do.

ANGEL: I don't think it was that guy's order that did that on May 6. Actually, it was more complicated. But, even if it was, can he do that and threaten the entire market? He woke up on Tuesday and said, I want to do this, it is reckless, but I don't really care about everybody else.

BRITTON: Then you go back and say, can Jerome Kerviel do that to Societe Generale when he was trading there?[17] Where do you stop in terms of saying the marketplace is a free market society? If the guy wants to sell 75,000 contracts, so be it.

---

[15] For background, see, Findings Regarding The Market Events of May 6, 2010. Report of the Staffs of the CFTC and SEC to the Joint Advisory Committee on Emerging Regulatory Issue, http://www.sec.gov/news/studies/2010/marketevents-report.pdf

[16] The "fat finger" refers to human mechanical error in entering a trade via key strokes. The error in this instance could be 75,000 rather than 75. The "fat finger" would have clumsily typed in three unintended zeroes.

[17] In 2010, Jerome Kerviel was found guilty of a €4.9bn trading loss at Societe Generale.

Then it comes down to a whole host of issues including risk management and controls, etc. But is it the exchange's responsibility to say that you can't sell 75,000 contracts?

ANGEL: Or the brokers in the middle of that execution?

BRITTON: I agree. If I am a client of the customer, I'm pulling my account. The guy just hatched up this order. The order should have been done over three days. He did it in 20 minutes! Has he done anything wrong in the marketplace? I don't think he has.

HOOPER: I understand where you are coming from Paul [pointing at Paul]. I can understand yours as well [pointing to audience]. The key issue here is, who is setting that speed limit? Who ultimately is the gatekeeper? Generally, these negative things happen, and then we have this backlash afterwards about what the speed limit should have been because something went wrong. I do understand both sides of the equation on this issue.

WALD: Marcus, we are asking the wrong question. It is not about speed. Dr. Angel is saying that the market isn't fast enough to deal with that destabilizing situation. In light of the fact that we are not fast enough, what do we do to stabilize the market, or at least to act more uniformly across all exchanges? That is why Accenture traded at a penny. It was because we ran into some half-failed scenario where the marketplace, from a structural perspective, didn't operate the way we wanted it to. And different exchanges had different rules at that time for what they do in that scenario.

HOOPER: Let me qualify the metaphor about speed. I am not thinking in the context of physical execution speed, I am thinking about the rules. Whether the rules are about the size of an engine in a car, or how big the car can be. In this context, it doesn't matter what the rule is. But there is some kind of constraint around the process – so, on another level, that is where circuit breakers come in. In other words, that is a type of constraint. I am not thinking about execution speed, *per se*.

SCHWARTZ (Baruch College): The Flash Crash was certainly a very accentuated and dramatic event. But little 'flash crashes' occur quite often. I think of this as a property (and I am looking at Jim Ross as I say this) of a continuous market. That is essentially how it works. There is a trade every time a buy meets a sell. The trades are typically bilateral. Now, when a buy meets a sell so quickly and it is eliminating orders from the book faster than replenishment orders can come in, where can you go in the absence of any other mechanism that puts brakes on the system? You go straight down. The buys disappeared and that is it. You can say what you want about high frequency and technology. It is a natural property, and technology is neutral. It simply depends on how it is used. Is it being used in this environment in a way that at times accentuates the complexities of the continuous market?

HOOPER The gentleman made a comment about feedback loops. Think of it in the same context. Did we not see these feedback loops every day? We just don't spot them because they are not so big.

CANGEMI: Maybe I am misinterpreting some of the questions and answers. But the market mechanics functioned well on May 6. It was the human intellect portion that could not respond fast enough to the price changes and data influx because they had programmed themselves and the tools they use to a different market matrix. That was a matrix derived from historical patterns of trading, which had not been seen before. When you talk about high-frequency trading firms, they all pulled out of the market on May 6 primarily because their algorithmic strategies told them to walk away when things look this dramatically different from past normal conditions. I can tell you this much, the high-frequency traders, sell-side, buy-side, every management person who had fiscal risk on May 6, have since been spending inordinate amounts of hours changing their strategies, whether algorithmic or manual, to be more in line with the time and speed of trading of May 6. They are also looking at the notion of how do we react, and how do we access the market during these conditions. This was a crash just like all the other crashes that we've had before, and each one has had its own distinct causes. Like in the past, we will look to identify the causes and to put corrective measures in place both structurally and from a regulator's perspective. The May 6 Crash was the most expedient to date.

Yes, you could say that there should be a speed limit. But limits don't prevent adverse conditions. We have speed limits in school zones, and there are other real-life examples as well. There is a speed limit on my father's block where he brought his brand new car home on Saturday morning. Then, on Saturday afternoon, a woman drove by his brand new car, obviously not keeping to the speed limit. She hit a pothole, blew out a tire and went through his new car with only 52 miles on it!

You can't stop the inherent mistake, and if it was a mistake, we don't really know. Did they truly want to wreck the market? Did they really need a risk adverse position that needed them to be out in 20 minutes? No one really knows. To put the speed limit there is great. After the fact, you can say that you broke the law and you caused risk. But the reality is, we all recognized May 6 as a market condition that we would like to fix or at least make more palatable. I know that we are – and I am sure that everyone else is as well – looking at strategies and solutions to help alleviate some of the stress from those days.

ROSS: At the end of the day, across the board, everyone looked at each other and said that they didn't do anything wrong in the aftermath of May 6. The market did function, and it operated the way it should. Trades went up as they are supposed to, and the market had a one-sided direction. No one necessarily took the blame. I feel that there is a lot of self-interest that drives market structure. Yet, we have a higher purpose here. I think a lot of us realize that our economy and our global infrastructure is based on how this market operates. It seized up on May 6. I don't think a penny a share for Accenture is right. I don't know whose fault it is. I don't think you can blame somebody. Maybe you can, but it is really a collection of elements.

Bob has often talked about the lighthouse concept, the idea that a community builds a lighthouse and everyone is able to use it. People rely on that lighthouse. In the context of May 6, you got your customers orders to the market. You processed the orders quickly. The LRPs kicked in.[18] My stop price logic did what it was supposed to do. But, at the end of the day, the market dropped like a stone, and then rebounded in about two minutes. And that is not a properly functioning market.

[18] This refers to the trading pause mechanism in the Liquidity Replenishment Points (LRPs) program operated by the New York Stock Exchange.

SCHACK: So Joe, should that lady's car have some mechanism built into it to keep her from going 52 miles an hour in a 25 mile an hour residential zone? Should there be more responsibility? I think the exchanges are handling this, but should responsibility be placed on brokers as well? A lot of the buy-side have these electronic tools on their desktop. They have these algos. The guys out in Kansas City might have said, Okay, I am going to press the button and it gets sold.[19] Well guess what, it doesn't happen that way! There are myriad things that happen after you press the button. In a lot of cases, the buy-side has the illusion but not the reality of control. They probably know less about how their orders are executed today than they did when they handed them over to Joe Cangemi on the floor of the exchange, or sent them to the old Knight Securities' market makers back in the day before today's market structure. That's one of the dual edge sword results that we get from technology.

CAROL COMERTON-FORDE (University of Sydney) From the Floor: There has been a lot of innovation since the enactment of Reg NMS[20] – mainly by the exchanges on fees and on speed. That's driven by the constraint imposed by the best price rule, and the trade-through rule in Reg NMS. To what extent can there be innovation in market structure when you are constrained by not trading through?

WALD: There are plenty of examples that I have been working on for years. And here they are: A lot of my colleagues on the sell-side are innovating, whether it is creating new algorithms for different asset classes, or creating algorithms that interact with multiple asset classes, or taking a look at the equity asset class and at segmenting that market into small-cap, mid-cap, and large-cap stocks. What can we do electronically my colleagues ask? Or, what can we do with this new infrastructure to enable us to trade the small-cap stocks electronically?

There is tremendous innovation that can still take hold in that space. Look at portfolio algorithms, or at pair's trading, or at lots of different things. Given the marketplace, the technology, and the speed that we now have, how can we best use that to our advantage as an innovator, or as an entrepreneur, to change the outcome in terms of a particular strategy? In other words, there are so many different strategies with different outcomes but lots of room to make the performance of those strategies better.

STEVEN SAX (FBN Securities) From the Floor: The system worked on May 6 from Joe Cangemi's point of view. I heard about Accenture trading at a penny a share.

---

[19] In its report on the Flash Crash, the CFTC and SEC report noted a skittish market environment prior to the Crash because of concern about European sovereign debt. However, the report cited a single sell order of 75,000 S&P E-mini contracts traded at the Chicago Mercantile Exchange as the catalyst for the Crash. Media reports cited the mutual fund Waddell & Reed in Kansas as the source of that sell order, which was valued at approximately $4.1 billion.

See, Kansas mutual fund at center of flash crash, Nelson D. Schwartz, *New York Times*, May 15, 2010. http://www.sfgate.com/business/article/Kansas-mutual-fund-at-center-of-flash-crash-3264771.php

[20] Regulation NMS, or National Market System, was enacted by the Securities and Exchange Commission in 2007 to foster competition among US exchanges and individual orders, and to promote fairness in price executions across all exchanges and platforms.

My feeling is that May 6 was a unique day and it was not an atypical market panic, or a market crash like we have had in the past. As Joe Wald mentioned, we have this fragmented market, all the different methodologies and different rules, and certain exchanges stopped trading, including the New York Stock Exchange when they had their order imbalances, specifically in the trading of Proctor & Gamble.

I agree with Joe Wald. You need some sort of regulation to oversee this fragmented market. I find it surprising that we are now waiting for the SEC to come up with the answers for all of this. It seems obvious that, when you have fragmentation in different exchanges in the same security, you need someone to oversee those markets.

ADAMS: A couple of weeks after the events of May 6, the IOSCO[21] annual conference was held in Montreal. There was much debate about what caused the Flash Crash, from flickering quotes and all the other things. Systemic risk then became one of the new global principals for global regulators looking at how to address market uncertainties. Global oversight was a cause of what happened on May 6. Consider the short-sale interventions around the world – some jurisdictions stepped in and others didn't step in. Regulators around the world reacted on May 6 in different ways – some imposed short-sale bans, and others did not. But what we need beyond that is some global oversight to provide a consistent approach in how we respond to market turmoil. The lack of global oversight caused some of the issues of May 6. As Joe said, people are repositioning their strategy to take advantage of the environment that now exists, warts and all. And that will always be the case. Market participants responded appropriately, demonstrating the dynamic nature of the market. Yes, there is an overarching requirement to see beyond individual instances.

BRITTON: Full disclaimer, I am not a technologist. I don't know if the system should have performed better than it did. If someone wants to get out of his position, what will the marketplace and the regulators allow him to do? This is where the difference of opinion comes in. If I want to sell 75,000 futures in 20 minutes and am comfortable with that, within my margin limits, then is it the prerogative of the exchanges to say no, that you can't do that? It is a healthy debate.

HOOPER: When I think about the way in which the London Stock Exchange has evolved, it does beg the question: If I want to travel at 1,000 miles an hour, why shouldn't I be allowed to? This is a consequence of regulation that has occurred, not just over years, but for many decades. We have ended up in an environment where we have order-driven markets. The whole point of that order-driven process is to democratize the market. I agree that there has been a systemic risk failure in the market. But the bigger picture is that this is a consequence of what has been going on for years.

CANGEMI: It was suggested that this Crash might have been different at another time under different market structure circumstances. The '87 Crash had almost all the same relevant behavior. Some broker/dealers and exchanges closed down, some shut down, some didn't answer their phones, and some didn't have an operational

[21] The International Organization of Securities Commissions. See Website, http://www.iosco.org/about/

answer to what was happening in '87. They couldn't clear or settle a trade. There was a commission established by the US government to provide solutions post-'87 so that we might have a better national market. The SEC stepped up after the May 6 Crash to provide the circuit breakers. After the '87 crash, the commission took a year to introduce any type of circuit breaker mechanism. Market-wide circuit breakers where instituted in 1988 and were only used once in 1997.

WALD: The backlash should not be against technology. Everyone has to be honest. There are certain limitations to a continuous market. They are fundamental to a continuous market and the only way to prevent it is to have a regulatory oversight that has the same rules harmonized across all market participants. Ten percent, five percent, whatever that number is. It is a number that everyone should eventually agree on. Harmonization of regulation is the key. It is not technology's fault. There is a fundamental limitation to a continuous market.

DAVID WEILD (Capital Markets Investment Partners) From the Floor: Why is there such hesitancy to blame the SEC and Congress for some of this? On the one hand, the regulators unleash an explosion in innovation and, on the other hand, because it is one interconnected market, it is their responsibility to set the rules of engagement. Things like stub quotes have been a problem going all the way back to the NASDAQ dealer markets.[22] People have complained about this. Professor Angel pointed out that we are transacting at the speed of light. We have been looking to vilify market participants. But with the explosion in innovation, have the regulators really kept up?

SCHACK: Great question. I don't think that they have. I would draw the contrast between what happens here and what happens in Europe. In Europe they introduced MIFID[23] two and one half years ago. In Europe, the regulators knew what they were letting loose on the market. They said this was going to create a lot of change, so let's revisit it. Let's make sure we look back and ask what has changed. Is everything we put into place appropriate? Let's assess what the market reactions have been and change course if we need to.

The forces of change have arguably been even more dramatic in the United States going back to '96 and '97 when the first elements of the new regulations that have transformed our market structure went into place. It's been a sort of emergency room reaction. When something really bad goes wrong, then we look at the regulations. There should be more regular examinations by the regulatory authorities on an ongoing basis of whether their rules and regulations have kept up with change. This process should be formalized and standardized, and not just be reactive.

ROSS: Having worked at the New York Stock Exchange, I have a different approach on rules and regulations. I spent 18 months getting the MatchPoint facility through the SEC regulatory process. I have differing views about it. To begin with,

---

[22] Stub quotes are bids for stocks near zero. For example, $0.01 bid for a stock trading at $25.00.

[23] MiFID, the Markets in Financial Instruments Directive was enacted as European Union law on November 1, 2007 to foster competition and investor protection. It harmonizes the regulation of financial services among EU member nations.

for exchanges that must compete, it takes too long to innovate. They need the ability to get their innovations to market quicker than they can do today. I will also say that I learned a hell of a lot more about my system. That was after I was pressed to answer questions about this system, an innovation that would ultimately be put into a very public, transparent environment.

I had to think really deeply about how the thing worked, and I had to get into the minutiae. There is cathartic value to the process, and ultimately there is value to the transparency that a regulator can promote. People need to know how operational transparency and process transparency works. I think about these two pulling forces – operational transparency and process transparency – and I believe that we can make improvements. That said, I stress that the SEC can improve on its processes. The agency is trying to keep up with an extremely fast moving environment. I wouldn't abandon the role of challenging it.

If a new ATS emerges, we want transparency along with it. We should certainly demand that. Right now, the American public finds non-displayed liquidity extremely discomforting. They don't understand it, as we saw in a recent *60 Minutes* segment.[24] There were some very simplistic terminologies used in that segment and America just does not understand this. We need to realize that. And we need to make this better and more transparent for those who need to understand it.

UNIDENTIFIED AUDENCE MEMBER: Can we revisit the "F" word, fragmentation, but from a different spin? Can we revisit it in terms of the regulatory structure in this country? Why haven't the CFTC and SEC been merged? Would things have been different with both the Flash Crash as well as other market structure issues, or is it over done to blame it on the regulatory structure?

SCHACK: I never underestimate the ability of Congress to get things wrong. The reason the CFTC and SEC weren't merged is political in nature.[25] They had some power to keep that from happening. However, a merger would have been the sensible approach.

As mentioned, ordinary folks just don't get this market structure stuff. They don't particularly want to get it. I hate to say this, it sounds elitist, but will they ever get it? We need to do a better job of trying to explain market structure to them. I don't think that market structure is the kind of issue that politicians can benefit from playing a role in, from really trying to understand how it works, and from finding the right answers. It is even more of an issue in the post-crisis environment. It could be an opportunity to look like they are striking a blow against the Wall Street fat cats, or finding the next bubble and reacting to stop it. In reality, they are not understanding the issues and they are potentially doing more harm than good.

CANGEMI: The SEC and CFTC are now working better together. FINRA has taken on a more global responsibility rather than the fragmented responsibility that

---

[24] See, Extra: How High Frequency Trading Grew. *60 Minutes*, CBS News www.cbsnews.com/video/watch/?id=6945166n

[25] For background, see, Avoiding the next big financial crisis, Jennifer Liberto, *CNNMoney*, June 8, 2009, http://money.cnn.com/2009/06/05/news/economy/financial_regulation/index.htm

they had at the start. The press and surrounding discussion have forced the parties to move in a more positive direction, or at least that is the direction we want them to move in.

ROSS: The SEC actually brought me in to discuss dark pools and non-displayed liquidity with their investigators in the division of enforcement. I don't think I am the only one who talked to these folks. They questioned different market participants, including the providers. Can they do better? Absolutely they can. Can they be more aggressive? Certainly, but they are trying to get a better grasp of what is going on here. I do think they have been reaching out, tapping other people with experience and expertise to give them insight. That is an important direction.

HOOPER: If I have one function in life, it is to match supply and demand. We have one remaining question.

BILL HARTS (Harts & Company)[26] From the Floor: Earlier someone pointed out that perhaps the buy-side should have more information, and that they should understand better how the different algorithms they use work. I would like to ask the panel, and especially the brokers, this question: Would you be willing, or does it make sense, to allow your buy-side clients to dig down into those algorithms? Dig down maybe to the point of letting them audit the code to really understand how they work?

CANGEMI: These discussions between brokers and their clients are already happening. Normalizing or standardizing the data points for that conversation will go a long way towards satisfying the massive customer base. The questions that they ask are so dramatically different, and what data points they are looking to capture and how they want to capture it, is a complicated matter. But, yes, brokers are more than willing to share information, at least the brokers I have been affiliated with. They are willing to share as much information as makes the customer comfortable. Remember, customers, like anyone else, only use what they are comfortable with. So you have to satisfy your customers by providing them with as much data as they can use without jeopardizing the integrity of your investment strategy. But there is a lot of work to be done on that front.

SCHACK: We do not have algorithms, and we are an agency shop. Brokers are starting to make more information available on how their algos work in relation to their executions. But, they will often do it in ways where, to Rob Shapiro's point from an earlier panel today, they just answer the questions that you ask and nothing more. And if you don't ask the right questions, and you don't have someone independent telling you which questions you should be asking, then you are probably not going to get all the information that you need. Brokers will figure out ways to tell you that they are doing the right thing when, in fact, they are routing your orders to the most convenient, cheapest execution venues – rather than to the ones where you will get the best execution.

---

[26] In June 2011, Bill Harts joined Thomson Reuters Markets as Chief Strategy Officer for Sales & Trading.

ROB RICHARDSON (Zicklin School of Business) From the Floor: I know in the connectivity world, the FIX world, that when you make a connection or change a connection, you do a lot of one on one testing. Do you think that it is time for the industry to do a lot more cross testing between smart order routers and between exchanges? It is possible that these exchange markets are a lot more coordinated and integrated than may have appeared to be the case on May 6.

CANGEMI: As noted, there are differences in the way the markets behaved on that day. But this does not necessarily apply to the communication network, or to the FIX protocols, and the connectivity between the players in the market, including the numerous brokers, 13 exchanges and 43 or so dark pools.

RICHARDSON: Can anything be done between these venues other than one on one testing?

CANGEMI: We have market-wide testing, especially with the implementation of Reg NMS. It was mandatory that anyone competing with regard to market structure had to adhere to that testing schedule, and reports were generated. I don't know how frequently you can do this, but system testing is occurring on a regular basis.

HOOPER: We have to stop it here. Thank you, panel and audience.

Chapter 6
Closing Remarks

Richard Ketchum, *Chairman and CEO, FINRA*

ROBERT SCHWARTZ: It is my great honor to introduce Rick Ketchum. As you all know, Rick is an outstanding highlight for this conference. His many admirers say Rick has a fantastic and extraordinary way of thinking about market structure. I agree. Rick, you really don't need any introduction with this kind of reputation. Welcome. (Applause)

RICHARD KETCHUM:

As I look out across this conference room at the sea of faces, my entire career is before me. At some point, my career has intersected with the various parts of our industry that are represented by people in this room. It is a little daunting, therefore, to stand up here as a regulator—and as a partially recovering market structure jock—to talk to this distinguished crowd. Especially after you have spent the day parsing the details of each excellent panel. But let me share a few thoughts. I want to give you a sense of how some of the issues tend to be looked at from a regulatory standpoint.

I understand your frustration in continually keeping up with regulation. But rest assured, the SEC and the CFTC have never been more interested in hearing from you. I can speak to that personally since my regulatory career was kicked off decades ago when I participated in a study of the options industry. There is nothing better for governmental agencies than to listen to and interact with a broad group of industry participants on issues of mutual interest. Indeed, it has been a long time since I have seen the SEC as well informed on a variety of trading issues as it clearly demonstrated in this latest joint CFTC-SEC study on the Flash Crash of May 6.[1]

You have been talking today about the numerous questions that arise from the Flash Crash alongside the gradual developments and evolutionary changes in the trading markets in the US and Europe. Let me add something. Putting aside

[1] Ketchum is referring to a study released by the Commodity and Futures Trading Commission and the US Securities and Exchange Commission. Findings Regarding The Market Events of May 6th, 2010, September 30, 2010. See, http://www.sec.gov/news/studies/2010/marketevents-report.pdf.

R.A. Schwartz et al. (eds.), *The Quality of Our Financial Markets: Taking Stock of Where We Stand*, Zicklin School of Business Financial Markets Series,
DOI 10.1007/978-1-4614-5592-9_6, © Springer Science+Business Media New York 2013

qualitative viewpoints, it seems to me that an interesting thing happened with how the markets operated on that fateful day. It stems from a conscious effort on the regulatory side, including on the part of the SEC, to enhance and encourage competition, to reduce transaction costs, and to increase transparency.[2] That's while the regulators continue to ensure market access for investors and competitors across a wide variety of liquidity venues. The result is an exceptionally competitive marketplace that provides a wide range of alternatives. Yet as the SEC and CFTC study shows, it also creates a very fragile environment in volatile times.[3] It creates fragility for a variety of reasons.

First, this competitive marketplace results in an exceptional degree of fragmentation. Fragmentation is increased because of the ability of individual firms to internalize orders within a range of execution facilities. For example, some are trying to work with institutional investors and hedge fund customers; some are internalizing their order flow directly.[4]

Today, 30 percent of the order flow, more or less, is executed outside of the exchange market environment. The other 70 percent is fragmented across a substantial number of exchanges. Of course, in normal circumstances, that occurs within a regulatory system that connects the various books of liquidity and provides executions and rules that ensure 'top of the book' trading.[5] On the other hand, the regulatory system doesn't require any particular approach in executing the rest of the book, particularly in volatile times.

Not surprisingly, the CFTC-SEC study also shows in an interesting way how the 30 percent handled by the internalization of individual firms seeking liquidity is moved about.[6] That is particularly acute at times when firms, through their electronic systems, effectively detect exactly what is happening in these volatile markets and whether they are operating at an informational disadvantage to other market participants.

Next, the exchanges – being totally commoditized – essentially have no leverage for encouraging market-maker obligations other than in a very minimalist effort, or

---

[2] For a more expansive viewpoint on this topic, read Ketchum's subsequent keynote at the Annual Conference of the Security Traders Association, Palm Beach. FL., October 13, 2011. http://www.finra.org/Newsroom/Speeches/Ketchum/P124661

[3] Findings Regarding The Market Events of May 6th, 2010, September 30, 2010. See, http://www.sec.gov/news/studies/2010/marketevents-report.pdf

[4] At the time of writing, US stock trading occurred on 10 public exchanges, 30-plus dark pools, and over 200 internalizing broker dealers. Many of the dark pools accommodated internalization by their owners. In excess of three quarters of the order flow executed through dark pools was thought to be internalized. Some 33% of NYSE volume and 25% of NASDAQ volume was reported off-exchange and it was mostly internalized order flow, according to industry calculations.

[5] The US equity markets are governed and regulated today by various regulations including Reg NMS. The "top of the book" refers to how the best electronically delivered price quotes, the so-called top-of-book orders, must be posted across all exchanges under the mandate of Reg NMS.

[6] See, Findings Regarding The Market Events of May 6th, 2010, September 30, 2010. http://www.sec.gov/news/studies/2010/marketevents-report.pdf

with respect to particular exchanges that choose to differentiate themselves in that way.[7] That kind of begins and ends with the New York Stock Exchange and some other exchanges to a limited extent.

Without ever pretending that market makers by themselves provided liquidity in extraordinary times – actually, they don't – I can say, however, that they do provide some level of continuity. Yet this has now disappeared, particularly at times when very few people have a strong view of market direction and of where trading volume is directionally moving, at low levels like today. I have not seen these low levels before in my 30-year career. Today, you have an even greater concentration of electronic trading volume that is highly dependent on algorithms. These are basically driving the market in both directions. That is neither good nor bad. It is just what you see in this environment.

Those algorithms in a rough way break down into two sets of strategies. One is fundamentally liquidity provision and spread advantaging. These algorithms are designed so that when volatility reaches a point where it does not fit the parameters of those algorithms, they trigger a computerized trading instruction for trading participants to withdraw from the market until some human trader decides that it is okay to enter the market again. Finally, the other piece is the opportunistic, more speculative programs. These algorithms look at the type of volatility in the market before sending a series of messages suggesting that it is a uniquely opportunistic time for the algorithmic trader from the standpoint of selling programs. As that liquidity is being withdrawn from the books, more substantial selling occurs. That selling has not tended to be vetted and rigorously analyzed, even as these algorithms and models have proliferated. Consequently, their design has not tended to spend a lot of time being concerned with the disruptive impacts of their opportunistic actions.[8]

That roughly describes the marketplace. It has great advantages and disadvantages. It is a market that deserves to be debated. The SEC is owed great credit for highlighting this kind of marketplace in their Concept Release.[9] There are no simple answers. However, a few conclusions are needed to instill confidence.

In the wake of the Flash Crash, I am pleased to say that we participated with the exchanges – and, by the way, with great leadership from the SEC – in developing rules in response to what occurred.[10] To that end, when you have a range of issues that make markets fragile, you need time outs. You need market pauses; and you need to err on the side of pauses even if that does impact the efficient operations of

[7] See, SEC Questions Trading Crusade as Market Makers Disappear, Nina Mehta, *Bloomberg*, September 13, 2010 http://www.bloomberg.com/news/2010-09-13/sec-second-guesses-its-stock-trading-crusade-as-u-s-market-makers-vanish.html

[8] See, Securities watchdog probes high-frequency trading firms: report, *Reuters*, March 23, 2012 http://news.yahoo.com/securities-watchdog-probes-high-frequency-trading-firms-report-063227979.html

[9] See, Concept Release on Equity Market Structure, January 14, 2010, http://www.sec.gov/rules/concept/2010/34-61358.pdf

[10] See, for example, FINRA Regulatory Notice 10–43, http://www.finra.org/Industry/Regulation/Notices/2010/P121634

markets. Maybe there is a way to change this approach and still encourage all the competition. As it operates now, pauses were a fundamental and necessary step in response to the Flash Crash. Indeed, I think it is a great thing today that such pauses, for example, have moved out across the Russell 1000.[11]

More importantly, pauses have been implemented with respect to a wide range of the ETFs. But they need to go further. With the exception of a few low-priced stocks and a few inactive stocks, they should go out across all of them. Everyone should take much comfort with securities in the Russell 1000 being included in the trading pause plan. Certainly with regards to the systemic risk, we are better off now than we were before.

What are the minimal steps that need to be taken? First, we ought to keep working to make sure the pauses are designed as best they can be. SEC Chairman Mary Schapiro is absolutely right to say that this requires a careful analysis of the pros and cons of a 'limit' approach, or of some combined limit and pause approach.[12] I give the SEC great credit for looking in that direction.

Limits obviously avoid the problems of single trades either stopping trading altogether, or printing outside of certain ranges and causing tension and confusion among investors. However, these limits are a harder approach than actual pauses. Deciding the reference point prices for these limits is somewhat challenging. A slew of trades reaching their limits creates the same risk of downward movement if you consider that algorithms are not designed to self-correct in the same way that a human trader might react in similar circumstances. Five seconds may have worked on the e-mini. The likelihood that it works on an individual stock basis is open to question.[13]

Yes, Bob, there is merit in the wonderful thing that you have lectured us about for years and years and provided great insight into. Indeed, there is a value to the

---

[11] See FINRA Regulatory Notice 10–30 http://www.finra.org/Industry/Regulation/Notices/2010/P122122

Two years after the Flash Crash, some commentators were critical of the regulatory measures taken to help prevent a similar occurrence again. For one thing, these pauses or circuit breakers to halt trading in stocks were seen as counterproductive in some instance. See, US 'flash crash' measures suffer delays. Telis Demos, Financial Times, May 6, 2012. http://www.ft.com/intl/cms/s/0/ee439fe6-96af-11e1-847c-00144feabdc0.html#axzz1vF32UV4n

Also, see, Overview, SIFMA http://www.sifma.org/issues/capital-markets/equity-markets/flash-crash/overview/

[12] Ketchum is referring to price limits on some stocks that would temporarily stop trading if they traded outside pre-defined limits. For a summary of SEC regulatory action in this matter, see, Two Years After Flash Crash, SEC Still Pursuing New Safeguards, Michael Peltz, http://www.institutionalinvestor.com/Article/3023836/Two-Years-After-Flash-Crash-SEC-Still-Pursuing-New-Safeguards.html

[13] "At 2:45:28 p.m., trading on the E-Mini was paused for five seconds when the CME Stop Logic Functionality was triggered in order to prevent a cascade of further price declines. In that short period of time, sell-side pressure in the E-Mini was partly alleviated and buy-side interest increased. When trading resumed at 2:45:33 p.m., prices stabilized and shortly thereafter, the E-Mini began to recover." Page 16, Findings Regarding The Market Events of May 6th, 2010, September 30, 2010. See, http://www.sec.gov/news/studies/2010/marketevents-report.pdf

equivalent of your single-priced auction (aka "call auction"), conveying to participants at times of market stress that the world has not ended. With a single-priced auction there is greater visibility of buy and sell interest and enhanced ability to find an appropriate single price. I think the SEC is absolutely right in this regard. We ought to explore and find a way to integrate this single-priced auction approach because it creates a tighter environment than pauses alone.

I would hate to see pauses lost. These are a critical mechanism. Market-maker obligations also need to be looked at again. They need to be looked at in a cross market[14] context because no single market, any longer, has any leverage to pose anything meaningful. I don't begin to suggest that market-maker obligations eliminate risk. But they do provide greater continuity. Market-maker obligations do lessen the risk of errors, and there is value in them. It is great that numerous market participants are stepping back and taking a hard look at that.

The joint CFTC-SEC study into the Flash Crash of May 6 also cries out for a careful look at the impact of fragmentation from entities that are not markets and do not have obligations. I come from NASDAQ. I also come from the New York Stock Exchange.[15] I feel very strongly both ways on this topic. I remember a time past when the NASDAQ operated a marketplace comprised of participants who internalized order flow. Now this is a little overstatement and, for the lawyers in the room, I recognize that it is not perfect. But, generally speaking, both from a regulatory standpoint and a customer expectation standpoint, these same participants who internalized did maintain quotes that were reasonably related to the market, and they traded at those quotes in some size.

It is not clear to me whether the present trade off, or a lack of trade off with respect to internalization that exists today, has been fully thought through. Would some model that differentiates market makers and participants operating in the market make sense from the internalized side? It may not be the right way to go. However, I do think that the removal of liquidity in difficult times, such as May 6, demonstrates that it would be good to take a look at the underlying expectations concerning how internalization was going to operate.[16] It would be good to ask whether there are lessons from the past, or from the future, that ought to be included.

---

[14] As defined by SEC in Findings Regarding The Market Events of May 6th, 2010, Sept. 30, 2010: "Cross-market strategies primarily focus on the contemporaneous trading of securities-related products in the futures and securities markets. The objective of these strategies is to capture temporary price differences between any two related products, but with limited or no exposure to subsequent price moves in those products."

[15] Ketchum is the former president of NASDAQ and was later the chief regulatory officer of the New York Stock Exchange, before serving as chief executive officer of NYSE Regulation. https://www.finra.org/AboutFINRA/Leadership/p019335

[16] "Notable in the trading activity of May 6 was the redirection of order flow by internalizing and preferencing firms to Exchange markets during the most volatile periods of trading. While these firms provide significant liquidity during normal trading periods, they provided little to none at the peak of volatility." P.12, Recommendations Regarding Regulatory Responses To The Market Events of May 6, 2010. Summary Report of the Joint CFTC-SEC Advisory Committee on Emerging Regulatory Issues. See, http://www.sec.gov/spotlight/sec-cftcjointcommittee/021811-report.pdf

Now let me talk a bit about the concerns of FINRA. I am glad the topic was raised in the last panel. At least from the standpoint of a broker-dealer sponsoring access to the marketplaces, a new and higher level of accountability is needed with respect to the algorithms that are used, most especially to the nuclear proliferation of algorithms over a wide range of participants. These algorithms include firms' and vendors' algorithms. FINRA and the New York Stock Exchange have stated as much in release after release. I am not suggesting that it is not difficult from a firm's standpoint to do it. However, if you are operating a broker-dealer, then you have a regulatory problem if you do not have a suitable analytical model with respect to how these algorithms operate. Therefore, we need to think of ways to accelerate accountability.

If that type of naked access[17] is still going to be permitted, the SEC has suggested proposals that would at least modify the practice. Finally, as one of the regulators who is also going to look more closely at this practice, I wish to state that it all comes down to what we've been discussing in great detail here today: The enhancement and betterment of our market structure as it evolves and improves in ways we could only have imagined a few short years ago. Clearly, such change is imperative for investors and the markets alike. We will all greatly benefit in the end.

Thank you.

[17] This so-called naked access permitted high-frequency traders and other market participants to buy and sell stocks on exchanges via a broker's computer code without any pre-trade checks or reviews. In November 2010, the Securities and Exchange Commission banned the practice.

MIX
Papier aus verantwortungsvollen Quellen
Paper from responsible sources
FSC® C105338

If you have any concerns about our products,
you can contact us on
ProductSafety@springernature.com

In case Publisher is established outside the EU,
the EU authorized representative is:
Springer Nature Customer Service Center GmbH
Europaplatz 3, 69115 Heidelberg, Germany

Printed by Libri Plureos GmbH
in Hamburg, Germany